Introduction

When I started freesciencelessons in 2013, I had one simple g
their understanding of science. When I was at school (and we're talking thirty years ago now), science was always my favourite subject. It's not surprising that I went on to become a science teacher. I know that many students find science challenging. But I really believe that this doesn't have to be the case. With patient teaching and a bit of hard work, any student can make amazing progress.

Back in 2013, I had no idea how big freesciencelessons would become. The channel now has nearly 70 million views from 192 countries with a total view time of over 300 years. I love to hear from the students who have patiently watched the videos and realised that they can do science after all, despite in many cases having little confidence in their ability. And just like in 2013, I still make all the videos myself (many students think that I have a staff of helpers, but no, it's just me).

This workbook is designed to complement the Chemistry 1 videos for the AQA specification. However, there is a huge amount of overlap with other exam boards and in the future I'll be making videos and workbooks for those as well. I've packed the workbook full of questions to help you with your science learning. You might decide to start at the beginning and answer every question in the book or you might prefer to dip in and out of chapters depending on what you want to learn. Either way is fine. I've also written very detailed answers for every question, again to help you really develop your understanding. You can find these by scanning the QR code on the front of the book or by visiting freesciencelessons.co.uk/c1tv1

Please don't think of science as some sort of impossible mountain to climb. Yes there are some challenging bits but it's not as difficult as people think. Take your time, work hard and believe in yourself. When you find a topic difficult, don't give up. Just go to a different topic and come back to it later.

Finally, if you have any feedback on the workbooks, you're welcome to let me know (support@freesciencelessons.co.uk). I'm always keen to make the workbooks better so if you have a suggestion, I'd love to hear it.

Good luck on your journey. I hope that you get the grades that you want.

Shaun Donnelly

Revision Tips

The first important point about revision is that you need to be realistic about the amount of work that you need to do. Essentially you have to learn two years of work (or three if you start GCSEs in Year 9). That's a lot of stuff to learn. So give yourself plenty of time. If you're very serious about getting a top grade then I would recommend starting your revision as early as you can. I see a lot of messages on Youtube and Twitter from students who leave their revision until the last minute. That's their choice but I don't think it's a good way to get the best grades.

To revise successfully for any subject (but I believe particularly for science), you have to really get into it. You have to get your mind deep into the subject. That's because science has some difficult concepts that require thought and concentration. So you're right in the middle of that challenging topic and your phone pings. Your friend has sent you a message about something that he saw on Netflix. You reply and start revising again. Another message appears. This is from a different friend who has a meme they want to share. And so on and so on.

What I'm trying to tell you is that successful revision requires isolation. You need to shut yourself away from distractions and that includes your phone. Nothing that any of your friends have to say is so critically important that it cannot wait until you have finished. Just because your friends are bored does not mean that your revision has to suffer. Again, it's about you taking control.

Remember to give yourself breaks every now and then. You'll know when it's time. I don't agree with people who say you need a break every fifteen minutes (or whatever). Everyone is different and you might find that your work is going so well that you don't need a break. In that case don't take one. If you're taking breaks every ten minutes then the question I would ask is do you need them? Or are you trying to avoid work?

There are many different ways to revise and you have to find what works for you. I believe that active revision is the most effective. I know that many students like to copy out detailed notes (often from my videos). Personally, I don't believe that this is a great way to revise since it's not really active. A better way is to watch a video and then try to answer the questions from this book. If you can't, then you might want to watch the video again (or look carefully at the answers to check the part that you struggled with).

The human brain learns by repetition. So the more times that you go over a concept, the more fixed it will become in your brain. That's why revision needs so much time because you really need to go over everything more than once (ideally several times) before the exam.

Revision Tips

I find with my students that flashcards are a great way to learn facts. Again, that's because the brain learns by repetition. My students write a question on one side and the answer on the other. They then practise them until they've memorised the answer. I always advise them to start by memorising five cards and then gradually adding in extra cards, rather than try to memorise fifty cards at once.

I've noticed over the last few years that more students do past paper practise as a way of revising. I do not recommend this at all. A past paper is what you do AFTER you have revised. Imagine that you are trying to learn to play the guitar. So you buy a guitar and rather than having lessons, you book yourself into a concert hall to give a performance. And you keep giving performances until you can play. Would you recommend that as a good strategy? I wouldn't. But essentially that's how lots of students try to revise. Yes by all means do practise papers (I've included a specimen paper in this book for you) but do them at the end when you've done all your revision. Past papers require you to pull lots of different bits of the specification together, so you should only do them when you are capable of that (ie when you've already done loads of revision).

A couple of final points ....

To reduce our environmental impact and to keep the price of this book reasonable, the answers are available online. Simply scan the QR code on the front or visit www.freesciencelessons.co.uk/c1tv1

There will be times when I decide to update a book, for example to make something clearer or maybe to correct a problem (I hope not many of those). So please keep an eye out for updates. I'll post them on Twitter (@UKscienceguy) and also on the FAQ page of my website. If you think that you've spotted a mistake or a problem, please feel free to contact me.

The Periodic Table of the Elements

1	2											3	4	5	6	7	0
																	4 **He** helium 2
7 **Li** lithium 3	9 **Be** beryllium 4											11 **B** boron 5	12 **C** carbon 6	14 **N** nitrogen 7	16 **O** oxygen 8	19 **F** fluorine 9	20 **Ne** neon 10
23 **Na** sodium 11	24 **Mg** magnesium 12											27 **Al** aluminium 13	28 **Si** silicon 14	31 **P** phosphorus 15	32 **S** sulfur 16	35.5 **Cl** chlorine 17	40 **Ar** argon 18
39 **K** potassium 19	40 **Ca** calcium 20	45 **Sc** scandium 21	48 **Ti** titanium 22	51 **V** vanadium 23	52 **Cr** chromium 24	55 **Mn** manganese 25	56 **Fe** iron 26	59 **Co** cobalt 27	59 **Ni** nickel 28	63.5 **Cu** copper 29	65 **Zn** zinc 30	70 **Ga** gallium 31	73 **Ge** germanium 32	75 **As** arsenic 33	79 **Se** selenium 34	80 **Br** bromine 35	84 **Kr** krypton 36
85 **Rb** rubidium 37	88 **Sr** strontium 38	89 **Y** yttrium 39	91 **Zr** zirconium 40	93 **Nb** niobium 41	96 **Mo** molybdenum 42	[98] **Tc** technetium 43	101 **Ru** ruthenium 44	103 **Rh** rhodium 45	106 **Pd** palladium 46	108 **Ag** silver 47	112 **Cd** cadmium 48	115 **In** indium 49	119 **Sn** tin 50	122 **Sb** antimony 51	128 **Te** tellurium 52	127 **I** iodine 53	131 **Xe** xenon 54
133 **Cs** caesium 55	137 **Ba** barium 56	139 **La*** lanthanum 57	178 **Hf** hafnium 72	181 **Ta** tantalum 73	184 **W** tungsten 74	186 **Re** rhenium 75	190 **Os** osmium 76	192 **Ir** iridium 77	195 **Pt** platinum 78	197 **Au** gold 79	201 **Hg** mercury 80	204 **Tl** thallium 81	207 **Pb** lead 82	209 **Bi** bismuth 83	[209] **Po** polonium 84	[210] **At** astatine 85	[222] **Rn** radon 86
[223] **Fr** francium 87	[226] **Ra** radium 88	[227] **Ac*** actinium 89	[261] **Rf** rutherfordium 104	[262] **Db** dubnium 105	[266] **Sg** seaborgium 106	[265] **Bh** bohrium 107	[277] **Hs** hassium 108	[268] **Mt** meitnerium 109	[271] **Ds** darmstadtium 110	[272] **Rg** roentgenium 111							

1 **H** hydrogen 1

Contents

Contents

Contents

Contents

Contents

Chapter 1: Atomic Structure and the Periodic Table

- State the definition of an element, mixture and compound.

- Use a chemical formula to state the elements in a molecule and the number of atoms of each element.

- Describe how a mixture can be separated by physical separation methods, including filtration, crystallisation, simple distillation, fractional distillation and paper chromatography.

- Describe the plum-pudding model of the structure of atoms and explain how the alpha-scattering experiment showed scientists that this model was incorrect.

- Describe the features of the nuclear model of atomic structure.

- Use the atomic number and the mass number for an element to determine the number of protons, neutrons and electrons.

- State what is meant by an isotope.

- Calculate the relative atomic mass for an element by using provided data on the different isotopes and their abundance.

- Assign electrons into their correct energy levels.

- Describe how scientists attempted to organise the elements into a periodic table and the steps that Mendeleev took to produce the first effective periodic table.

- Describe how the modern periodic table is different from the periodic table developed by Mendeleev.

- Explain why group 0 noble gases are unreactive and describe how their boiling points depend on their relative atomic masses.

- Describe how metals react to form positive ions.

- Describe how group 1 alkali metals react with oxygen, chlorine and water and explain why group 1 metals get more reactive moving down the group.

- Describe how group 7 halogens form diatomic molecules and how the melting and boiling points change moving down the group.

- Describe how group 7 elements react with non-metals and metals.

- Explain why group 7 elements get less reactive moving down the group and how a more reactive halogen can displace a less reactive halogen from its compounds.

- Describe the properties of transition elements.

Elements, Compounds and Mixtures

1. The periodic table shows us the elements.

a. Approximately how many elements have been discovered? Circle the correct answer.

(10)   (100)   (1000)

b. Which of the following is true about the atoms in an element?

All of the atoms in an element are different	All of the atoms in an element are the same	In some elements the atoms are all the same but in others they are all different

c. The diagrams below show the atoms in three different substances.

Which of the diagrams could show an element and which could not?

In each case explain your answer in the space next to the diagram.

d. Methane is a compound with the formula CH_4.

Explain why we cannot find methane on the periodic table.

e. A student wrote the symbol for cobalt as CO.

Explain why this is incorrect and what this actually shows.

2. The definition of a compound is shown below.

> A compound contains two or more different elements chemically combined in a fixed proportion

a. Ethane is a compound with the formula C_2H_6.

Use the example of ethane to explain what is meant by the words "fixed proportion".

b. Magnesium sulfide is a compound with one atom of magnesium chemically combined with one atom of sulfur.

Explain why the formula of magnesium sulfide is MgS and not MgS_2.

c. What can we say about the properties of a compound compared to the properties of the elements that the compound is made from?

> Quite similar

> The same

> Totally different

d. How do we separate the elements in a compound?

e. All of the following are molecules but only some are compounds.

In each case, state whether the molecule is a compound and explain your answer.

O_2

$AlCl_3$

Br_2

C_2H_6

f. If we want to separate a mixture, then we can use a physical technique rather than a chemical reaction.

State three examples of physical separation techniques.

Interpreting a Chemical Formula

1. Interpreting a chemical formula is an essential skill for GCSE Chemistry.

a. State the number of atoms of each element in the following compounds.

KCl

Number of potassium atoms =

Number of chlorine atoms =

Na_2O

Number of sodium atoms =

Number of oxygen atoms =

$CaSO_4$

Number of calcium atoms =

Number of sulfur atoms =

Number of oxygen atoms =

b. Use the periodic table to identify the elements in the compounds below.

Then use the formula to work out the numbers of atoms of each element.

$LiNO_3$

$FeCO_3$

NH_4NO_3

c. The formulas shown below have brackets.

Work out the elements and the number of atoms of each element.

$Ca(OH)_2$

$(NH_4)_2SO_4$

Filtration and Crystallisation

1. Filtration and crystallisation are often used to separate substances in chemistry.

Complete the following paragraph using the words below.

reduction   **chemical**   **mixture**   **physical**   **compound**

Both filtration and crystallisation are examples of _____ separation techniques.

We use these to separate the different parts of a _____ .

To separate the elements in a _____ we need to use a _____ reaction

such as _____ or electrolysis.

2. Calcium carbonate is a solid compound.

The formula for calcium carbonate is shown on the right.

$$CaCO_3 \, (\underline{\hphantom{xx}})$$

a. Write the state symbol for solid calcium carbonate in the space.

b. Calcium carbonate is insoluble in water.

Explain what is meant by this.

c. A mixture of calcium carbonate and water was filtered.

Draw an arrow from each label to the correct part of the diagram.

filter paper

filter funnel

calcium carbonate

water

d. The filtrate is what passes through the filter paper.

What is the filtrate in this case?

3. Magnesium chloride is a solid compound with the formula $MgCl_2$.

Magnesium chloride is soluble in water.

a. Select the correct formula to show magnesium chloride dissolved in water.

$MgCl_2 {}_{(g)}$ $MgCl_2 {}_{(aq)}$ $MgCl_2 {}_{(s)}$ $MgCl_2 {}_{(l)}$

b. Filtration cannot be used to separate magnesium chloride from water.

Explain why not.

c. An aqueous solution of magnesium chloride was left for several days.

The diagrams below show before and after.

Write the formula for magnesium chloride including state symbols in the spaces.

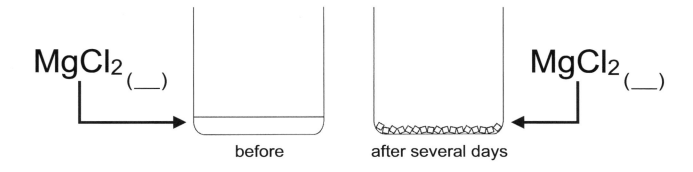

before   after several days

d. Crystallisation is a physical separation technique.

Explain how we can tell this from the diagram above.

e. We could speed up crystallisation by heating.

Explain why speeding up crystallisation by heating is not always a good idea.

Simple Distillation

1. Simple distillation separates a liquid from a solid, when we want to keep the liquid.

a. The diagram shows the apparatus used for simple distillation. Label the diagram using the words below.

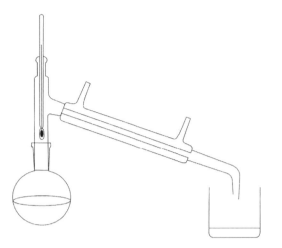

liquid + dissolved solid

condenser

cold water in

water out

thermometer

b. The following diagrams show the stages in simple distillation. Describe what is taking place in each stage.

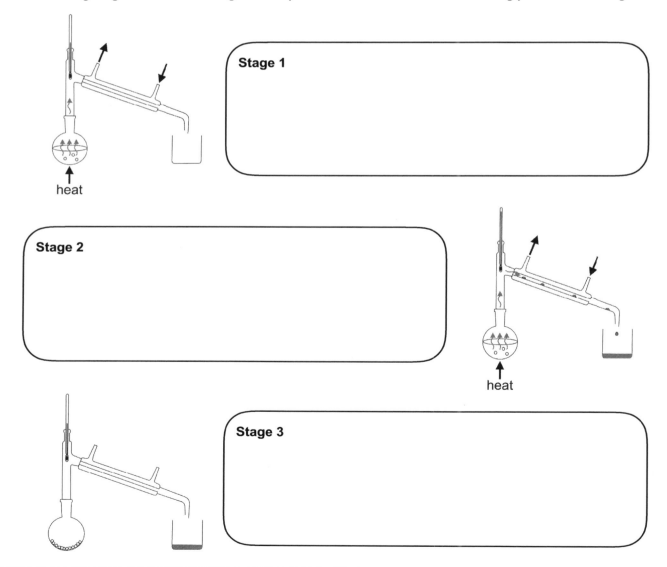

Stage 1

Stage 2

heat

Stage 3

Fractional Distillation

1. Fractional distillation is used to separate a mixture of different liquids.

a. For fractional distillation to work, the boiling points of the liquids must be (circle the correct answer) ...

| The same | Different |

b. Label the diagram for fractional distillation using the words below.

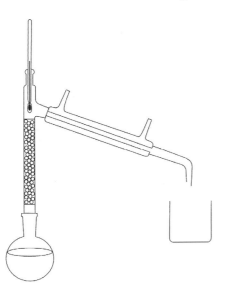

mixture of liquids

condenser

cold water in

water out

thermometer

fractionating column

2. The table shows the boiling points of three liquids.

A student tried to separate a mixture of these liquids using fractional distillation.

They found that the temperature on the thermometer rose initially and then stayed constant for several minutes.

During this time, the student used a beaker to collect the chemical from the condenser.

Chemical	Boiling point (°C)
A	130
B	68
C	120

a. Predict the temperature on the thermometer while it was constant.

Explain your answer.

b. After several minutes, the temperature began to increase.

Describe what was happening during this period.

c. The student found that two of the chemicals were hard to separate.

Suggest which two chemicals and explain your answer.

Paper Chromatography

1. Paper chromatography can be used to separate a mixture of soluble substances.

a. Explain why paper chromatography is an example of a physical separation technique.

b. In paper chromatography which parts are the stationary phase and the mobile phase?

> **Stationary phase =**

> **Mobile phase =**

c. Explain why some chemicals move further up the paper than other chemicals.

You should refer to the attraction between the chemicals and the stationary phase.

---

2. A student used paper chromatography to see if two different pens contained either a pure colour or a mixture.

Her results are shown on the right.

a. Explain why the student drew the starting line in pencil rather than pen.

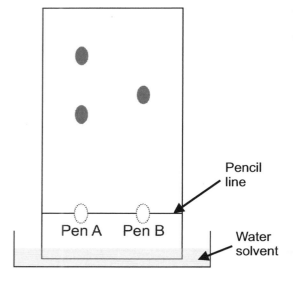

Pencil line

Pen A   Pen B

Water solvent

b. The student said:

"Pen A contained two colours and pen B contained only one colour. The two pens had a colour in common."

Was the student correct? Explain your answer.

c. From this experiment, the student could not be certain that pen B contains only one pure colour.

What could she do to check that?

Alpha-Scattering Experiment

1. One of the first models suggested for the structure of atoms was called the plum-pudding model.

a. Before the plum-pudding model, what did scientists believe about the structure of atoms?

b. How did the discovery of electrons change the scientists' ideas about the structure of atoms?

2. One of the diagrams below shows the correct version of the plum-pudding model.

State which diagram is correct and then explain why the other two are wrong.

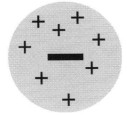

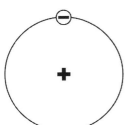

3. To see if the plum-pudding model was correct, scientists carried out the alpha-scattering experiment.

a. Describe what the scientists did in the alpha-scattering experiment.

Exam tip: Make sure that you learn the stages of the alpha-scattering experiment.

b. The results of the experiment are shown below.

Next to each finding, explain what this told the scientists about the structure of atoms.

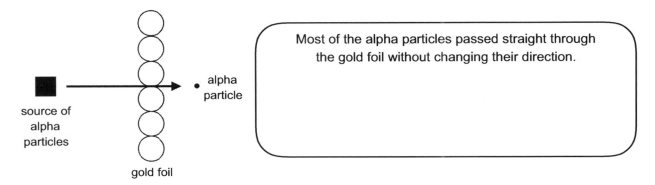

Most of the alpha particles passed straight through the gold foil without changing their direction.

Sometimes an alpha particle was deflected (changed its direction).

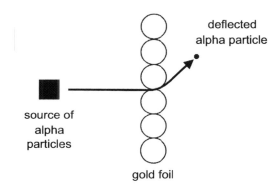

Sometimes an alpha particle bounced straight back towards the source.

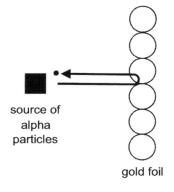

c. What was the name of the model of atomic structure that scientists developed from the alpha-scattering experiment?

The Nuclear Model

1. The results of the alpha-scattering experiment helped scientists to develop the nuclear model of atomic structure.

a. Use the words below to complete the description of the nuclear model of atomic structure.

electrons   **mass**   **positive**   **space**

In the nuclear model, most of an atom is simply empty _____ . In the centre

we have a _____ nucleus that contains most of the _____ of the

atom. Around the edge, we find negative _____ .

b. How did Niels Bohr's work improve the nuclear model?

c. Why did scientists accept Niels Bohr's proposal?

d. What did scientists discover about the positive charge of the nucleus?

e. What did James Chadwick discover about the nucleus?

2. Label the diagram below of the nuclear model of atomic structure.

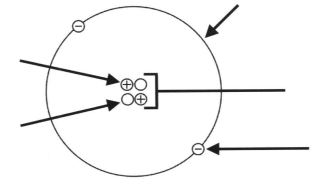

3. The diagram shows an atom of the element lithium.

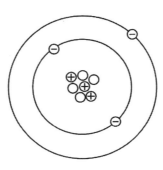

a. Using the information shown in the diagram, explain why lithium atoms have no overall charge.

b. Explain why the number of neutrons has no effect on the total charge of the atom.

4. You need to learn the key features of particles in an atom.

a. What is the typical radius of an atom?

Circle the correct answer.

1×10^{-8} m 1×10^{-9} m 1×10^{-10} m

b. How many times smaller is the radius of the nucleus than the radius of an atom?

| less than 1 / 1 000th the radius of the atom | less than 1 / 5 000th the radius of the atom | less than 1 / 10 000th the radius of the atom |

c. What is meant by the relative charge of a particle?

d. Complete the table to show the relative charges and relative masses of protons, neutrons and electrons.

Particle	Relative Charge	Relative Mass
Proton		
Neutron		
Electron		

Exam tip: many students confuse relative charge and relative mass. Make sure that you learn them.

Atomic Number and Mass Number

1. The symbol for every element has an atomic number and a mass number.

The symbol for the element fluorine is shown below.

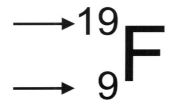

Exam tip: Remember that the mass number is always the larger of the two numbers.

a. Label the atomic number and mass number for fluorine.

b. What does the atomic number tell us about the particles in the nucleus?

c. From the above symbol for fluorine, how can we tell that the number of electrons is the same as the number of protons?

d. How do we use the atomic number and mass number to calculate the number of neutrons?

---

2. The atomic number and mass number for six elements are shown below.

Work out the number of protons, neutrons and electrons for the elements shown.

$^{27}_{13}$Al

protons = _____

neutrons = _____

electrons = _____

$^{65}_{30}$Zn

protons = _____

neutrons = _____

electrons = _____

$^{31}_{15}$P

protons = _____

neutrons = _____

electrons = _____

$^{88}_{38}$Sr

protons = _____

neutrons = _____

electrons = _____

$^{108}_{47}$Ag

protons = _____

neutrons = _____

electrons = _____

$^{45}_{21}$Sc

protons = _____

neutrons = _____

electrons = _____

3. Oxygen atoms have three main versions.

These are shown below.

$$^{16}_{8}O \qquad ^{17}_{8}O \qquad ^{18}_{8}O$$

protons = _____

neutrons = _____

electrons = _____

protons = _____

neutrons = _____

electrons = _____

protons = _____

neutrons = _____

electrons = _____

a. Determine the numbers of protons, neutrons and electrons for the different atoms of oxygen.

Write these in the spaces above.

b. These are different isotopes of oxygen.

What is meant by the word isotope?

c. Explain why isotopes have the same atomic number but different mass numbers.

---

4. Two different ions are shown below.

$$^{32}_{16}S^{2-} \qquad ^{40}_{20}Ca^{2+}$$

protons = _____

neutrons = _____

electrons = _____

protons = _____

neutrons = _____

electrons = _____

Exam tip: positive ions have lost electrons whereas negative ions have gained electrons

a. What is meant by an ion?

b. Work out the numbers of protons, neutrons and electrons for each ion.

c. Explain in terms of electrons how the ions above were formed.

Relative Atomic Mass

1. What is meant by the relative atomic mass for an element?

2. The relative atomic mass takes into account the abundance of each isotope.

What do scientists mean by the word abundance?

3. We calculate relative atomic mass using the equation below.

$$\text{Relative atomic mass} = \frac{\left(\begin{array}{c}\text{mass} \\ \text{number of} \\ \text{isotope 1}\end{array} \times \begin{array}{c}\text{percent} \\ \text{abundance of} \\ \text{isotope 1}\end{array}\right) + \left(\begin{array}{c}\text{mass} \\ \text{number of} \\ \text{isotope 2}\end{array} \times \begin{array}{c}\text{percent} \\ \text{abundance of} \\ \text{isotope 2}\end{array}\right)}{100}$$

Calculate the relative atomic masses of the following elements.

State all your answers to 1 decimal place.

$^{10}_{5}B$ percent abundance = 20%   Relative atomic mass of boron =

$^{11}_{5}B$ percent abundance = 80%

$^{63}_{29}Cu$ percent abundance = 69%   Relative atomic mass of copper =

$^{65}_{29}Cu$ percent abundance = 31%

$^{191}_{77}Ir$ percent abundance = 37%   Relative atomic mass of iridium =

$^{193}_{77}Ir$ percent abundance = 63%

Electron Energy Levels

1. In the exam, you could be asked to represent the electronic structure of any of the first twenty elements (up to Calcium).

The electronic structure for the element Beryllium is shown below.

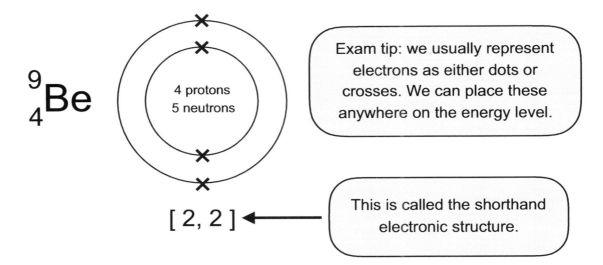

$^{9}_{4}$Be

4 protons
5 neutrons

Exam tip: we usually represent electrons as either dots or crosses. We can place these anywhere on the energy level.

[2, 2] ◀—— This is called the shorthand electronic structure.

a. State the maximum number of electrons that can be held in each energy level.

b. How does the electronic structure of Beryllium tell us that it must be in group 2?

c. Complete the diagrams for the following two elements.

$^{12}_{6}$C

_____ protons
_____ neutrons

[___]

Group = _____

$^{27}_{13}$Al

_____ protons
_____ neutrons

[___]

Group = _____

2. The diagrams below show two ions.

Complete the diagrams to show the energy levels and the shorthand electronic structures.

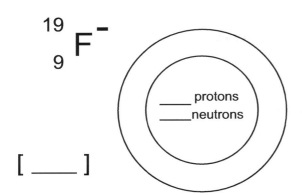

$^{19}_{9}F^{-}$

_____ protons
_____ neutrons

[_____]

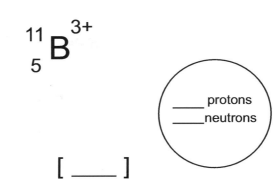

$^{11}_{5}B^{3+}$

_____ protons
_____ neutrons

[_____]

3. The diagrams below contain mistakes in their electronic structures.

Write the correct versions in the spaces.

$^{31}_{15}P$

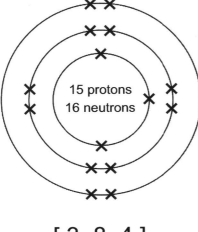

15 protons
16 neutrons

[3, 8, 4]

$^{31}_{15}P$

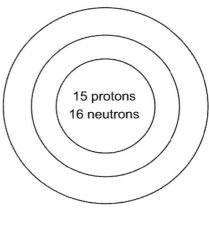

15 protons
16 neutrons

[   ]

$^{16}_{8}O^{2-}$

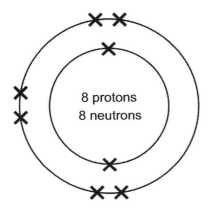

8 protons
8 neutrons

[2, 6]

$^{16}_{8}O^{2-}$

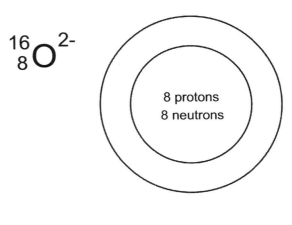

8 protons
8 neutrons

[   ]

Development of the Periodic Table

1. In the modern periodic table, elements are arranged by atomic number.

a. What do scientists call the columns in the periodic table?

Exam tip: This is another example of how a scientific model developed over time and is a very common exam question

b. Complete the paragraph using the words below.

chlorine   **reactive**   **sodium**   **non-metals**   **properties**

The periodic table is "periodic" because we find elements with similar _____ at

regular intervals. For example, group 1 elements consist of highly _____ metals

such as lithium and _____. Group 7 elements consist of high reactive

_____ such as fluorine and _____.

c. What can we say about the reactivity of elements in the same group of the periodic table?

d. Johann Dobereiner was one of the first scientists to notice patterns between the elements.
What did he notice?

2. The scientist John Newlands also looked for patterns in the elements.

He ordered the elements by increasing atomic weight. This is shown below.

Li	Be	B	C	N	O	F
Na	Mg	Al	Si	P	S	Cl
K	Ca					

Exam tip: Dobereiner and Newlands are not mentioned in the specification. But you could be given information on their discoveries in the exam and asked questions on them.

a. What pattern did Newlands notice when he ordered the elements like this?

b. Give an example of one of Newlands' octaves in the table above.

c. What was the main problem with Newlands' octaves?

3. The Russian scientist Dmitri Mendeleev developed the modern periodic table.

Mendeleev also arranged the elements in order of increasing atomic weight.

A version of his periodic table is shown below.

1
H

7	9			11	12	14	16	19
Li	Be			B	C	N	O	F

23	24			27	28	31	32	35.5
Na	Mg			Al	Si	P	S	Cl

39	40					75	79	80
K	Ca	Transition metals				As	Se	Br

85	88			115	119	122	128	127
Rb	Sr			In	Sn	Sb	Te	I

Property	Mendeleev's prediction	Germanium
Atomic mass	72	72.61
Density (g/cm³)	5.5	5.35
Melting point (°C)	high	947
Colour	grey	grey

a. Unlike Newlands, Mendeleev was happy to switch the order of elements if their properties did not match other elements in the same group.

State two elements which have been switched in Mendeleev's table above.

b. Mendeleev also left gaps in his periodic table. Explain why he did this.

c. Mendeleev realised that an element in the same group as silicon had not been discovered. He used his periodic table to predict the properties of the missing element. Several years later, the element germanium was discovered.

Mendeleev's predictions and the actual properties are shown in the table above.

Use the table above to explain why this prediction made other scientists accept that Mendeleev's table was correct.

d. State two ways that the modern periodic table is different from Mendeleev's.

e. When Mendeleev developed his table, protons had not been discovered.

Mendeleev ordered the elements by atomic weight.

What was the problem with ordering the elements by atomic weight?

Group 0

1. The first five elements of group 0 are shown on the left.

4 **He** helium 2	
20 **Ne** neon 10	
40 **Ar** argon 18	
84 **Kr** krypton 36	
131 **Xe** xenon 54	

a. What name do scientists give to the group 0 elements?

Circle the correct box.

> The
> halogens

> The alkali
> metals

> The noble
> gases

b. Why did group 0 not feature in the original periodic table developed by Dmitri Mendeleev?

c. Complete the following sentence by inserting the correct word.

> Atoms are stable when they have a _____ outer energy level

d. Use the diagram of group 0 above to draw the electronic structures of helium, neon and argon.

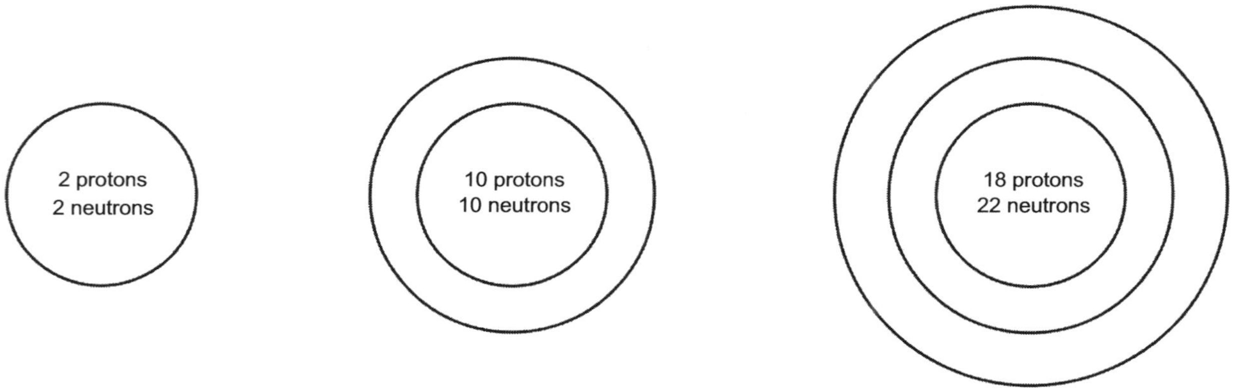

2 protons
2 neutrons

10 protons
10 neutrons

18 protons
22 neutrons

helium   neon   argon

e. Use the diagrams above to explain why the noble gases do not react with other elements.

2. The boiling points of the group 0 elements are shown in the table.

Group 0 element	Relative Atomic Mass	Boiling point (°C)
Helium	4	-269
Neon	20	-246
Argon	40	-186
Krypton	84	....
Xenon	131	-108
Radon	222	-62

a. Room temperature is 20°C.

Use the data in the table to explain why all of the group 0 elements are gases at room temperature.

b. Plot the boiling points on the graph paper below and draw a straight line of best fit through the points.

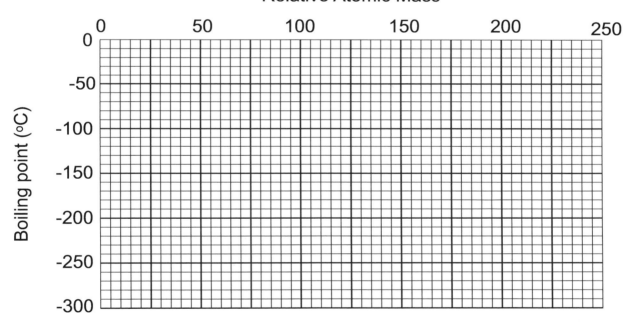

Relative Atomic Mass

c. Describe the link between the relative atomic mass and the boiling point of the group 0 elements.

d. Use the graph to estimate the boiling point of Krypton.

Boiling point of Krypton = _____ °C

Metals

1. Most of the elements in the periodic table are metals.

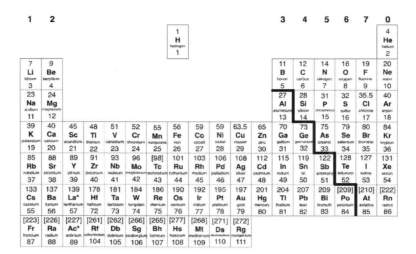

a. Whereabouts in the periodic table do we find the following:

> Metals

> Non metals

b. Whereabouts do we find the most reactive metals on the periodic table?

c. Where do we find the transition metals?

d. What can we say about the reactivity of the transition metals compared to the reactivity of the metals in groups 1 and 2?

e. How do metals react in terms of electrons? (select the correct answer)

> Metals share electrons

> Metals gain electrons

> Metals lose electrons

f. Explain in terms of their outer energy level why metals react like this?

2. When metals react, they form positive ions.

a. Explain in terms of electrons and protons why metals form positive ions.

b. Complete the diagrams to show the electronic structures of the metal ions.

Beryllium atom   Beryllium ion

The Beryllium ion has the same electronic structure as the noble gas_____

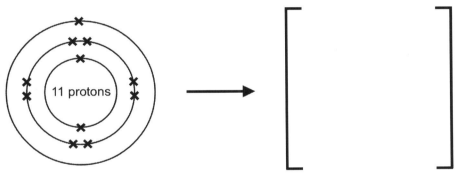

Sodium atom   Sodium ion

The Sodium ion has the same electronic structure as the noble gas_____

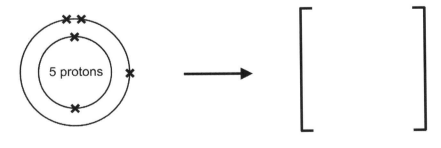

Boron atom   Boron ion

The Boron ion has the same electronic structure as the noble gas_____

c. Now write the charge on the top right hand corner of each ion.

d. For each ion, work out which noble gas has the same electronic structure and write in the space above.

Group 1 Metals

7 **Li** lithium 3
23 **Na** sodium 11
39 **K** potassium 19
85 **Rb** rubidium 37
133 **Cs** caesium 55

1. The first five elements of group 1 are shown on the left.

a. What name do scientists give to the group 1 elements?

Circle the correct box.

The halogens	The alkali metals	The noble gases

b. The diagram below shows the electronic structure of the element lithium.

Complete the diagram by drawing the electronic structure of sodium and potassium.

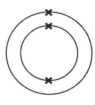

Lithium

[2, 1]

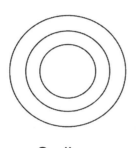

Sodium

[   ]

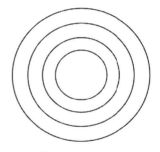

Potassium

[   ]

c. Complete the sentences by selecting the correct words.

The elements in group 1 have all got
| one |
| seven |
| eight |
electron in their outer energy level.

Group 1 elements are
| very hard |
| quite hard |
| soft |
and can be cut with a knife.

Group 1 elements are shiny but become dull as they react with
| nitrogen |
| oxygen |
| air |
.

2. You need to understand how group 1 elements react with oxygen.

a. Complete the word equations for the reaction of group 1 metals with oxygen.

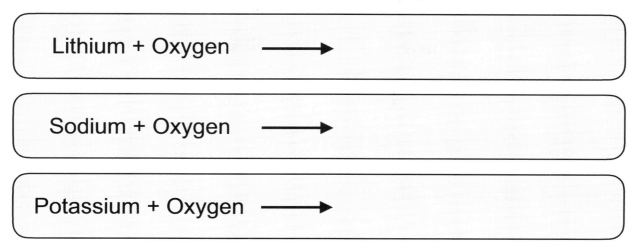

Lithium + Oxygen ⟶

Sodium + Oxygen ⟶

Potassium + Oxygen ⟶

b. What happens to the reactivity of the elements as we move down group 1? Circle the correct box.

| The elements get less reactive | The reactivity does not change | The elements get more reactive |

c. The diagram below shows the reaction between lithium and oxygen.

Complete the diagram to show the ions produced and the overall charge on each ion.

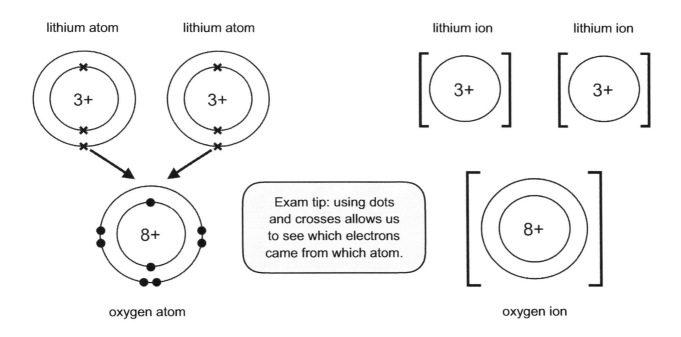

lithium atom   lithium atom   lithium ion   lithium ion

3+   3+   [3+]   [3+]

8+   Exam tip: using dots and crosses allows us to see which electrons came from which atom.   [8+]

oxygen atom   oxygen ion

d. Explain in terms of protons and electrons why the oxygen ion has a charge of 2 negative.

e. Explain why two lithium atoms react with one oxygen atom.

f. The formula of lithium oxide is Li_2O. Write the formula for sodium oxide and potassium oxide below.

sodium oxide	potassium oxide	Exam tip: All group 1 metals react in a similar way. This is because they have one electron in their outer energy level.

g. The equation for the reaction between lithium and oxygen is shown below.

Balance the equation by inserting a large number into the space.

$$4Li \quad + \quad O_2 \quad \longrightarrow \quad \underline{}Li_2O$$

h. Now write the balanced equation for the reaction between sodium and oxygen.

---

3. The reaction between lithium and chlorine is shown below.

a. Complete the diagram to show the ions produced and the overall charge on each ion.

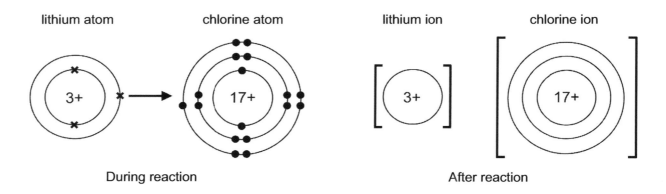

lithium atom	chlorine atom	lithium ion	chlorine ion
3+	17+	3+	17+

During reaction   After reaction

b. What can we say about the outer energy levels of the ions produced?

c. The equation for the reaction between lithium and chlorine is shown below.

Balance the equation by inserting a large number into the space.

$$\underline{}Li \quad + \quad Cl_2 \quad \longrightarrow \quad 2LiCl$$

4. A scientist added a piece of lithium to water containing some universal indicator. The equations for this reaction are shown below.

lithium + water $\longrightarrow$ lithium hydroxide + hydrogen

2 Li + 2 H_2O $\longrightarrow$ 2 LiOH + H_2

> Exam tip: Make sure you learn the reaction of group 1 metals with water.

a. The scientist made two observations. Use the equation above to explain these.

> effervescence

> universal indicator turned purple

b. The scientist then added a piece of sodium and then a piece of potassium.

In terms of reactivity, how would these reactions be different to lithium?

---

5. The electronic structures of lithium, sodium and potassium are shown below.

Use these to explain why the group 1 elements get more reactive down the group.

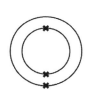

lithium

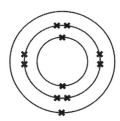

sodium

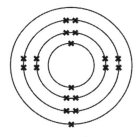

potassium

distance   **electron**   **shielded**   **attracted**   **reactive**

When group 1 elements react, they all lose one _____ from their outer energy level.

Moving down group 1, the outer electron is less _____ to the nucleus and is easier to

lose. This is because there is a greater _____ between the positive nucleus and the outer

electron. Also, the outer electron is _____ from the nucleus by the internal energy levels.

Because of this, the elements get more _____ moving down group 1.

Group 7 Part 1

19
F
fluorine
9
35.5
Cl
chlorine
17
80
Br
bromine
35
127
I
iodine
53
[210]
At
astatine
85

1. Group 7 elements form many compounds in Chemistry.

a. What name do scientists give to the group 7 elements?

Circle the correct box.

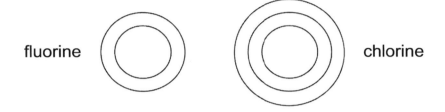

| The noble gases | The alkali metals | The halogens |

b. Use the diagram on the left to show the electronic structures of fluorine and chlorine.

fluorine ◯ ◎ chlorine

c. Use the above diagram to explain why all of the elements in group 7 react in a similar way.

---

2. All of the halogens form molecules with two atoms. Scientists call these diatomic molecules.

a. Complete the diagram below to show how two atoms of fluorine react to form a fluorine molecule (F_2).

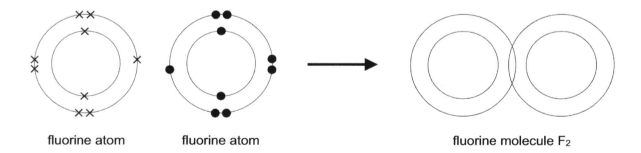

fluorine atom   fluorine atom   fluorine molecule F_2

b. Explain in terms of electrons why halogens form diatomic molecules.

c. Halogen molecules contain a single covalent bond.

Label the covalent bond on the fluorine molecule above.

3. The melting and boiling points of the halogens change as the relative molecular mass increases. This is shown on the graph below.

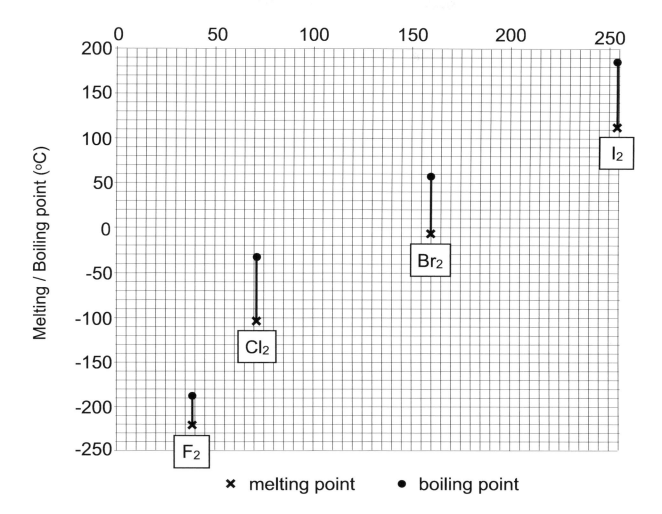

a. Describe how the melting points and boiling points change with relative molecular mass.

b. Explain how the graph shows that fluorine and chlorine are gases at room temperature (20°C).

c. What is the physical state of iodine at room temperature (solid, liquid or gas)?
Explain your answer.

Group 7 Part 2

1. When halogens react with other non-metal atoms, they form covalent compounds.

Complete the diagram below to show the formation of the covalent compound hydrogen chloride.

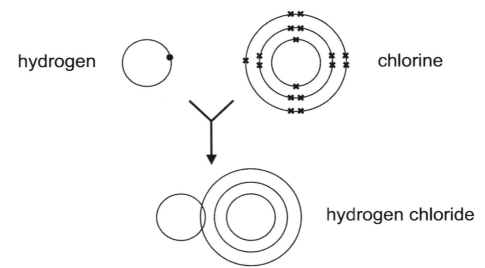

hydrogen

chlorine

hydrogen chloride

2. When halogens react with metal atoms, they form ionic compounds.

a. Complete the diagram below to show the formation of the ionic compound magnesium fluoride.

You will need to draw the electronic structures and the charges of the ions produced.

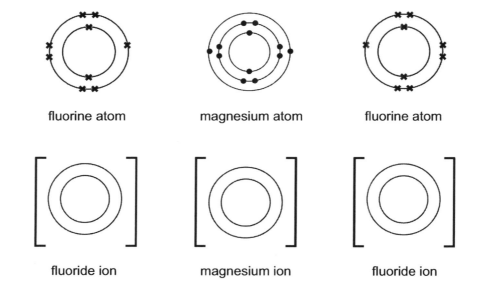

fluorine atom

magnesium atom

fluorine atom

fluoride ion

magnesium ion

fluoride ion

b. Which of the following is the correct formula for magnesium fluoride?

Explain your answer.

$$MgF \qquad\qquad Mg_2F \qquad\qquad MgF_2$$

Group 7 Part 3

1. The electronic structures of fluorine and chlorine are shown below.

Use these to explain why the group 7 elements get less reactive down the group.

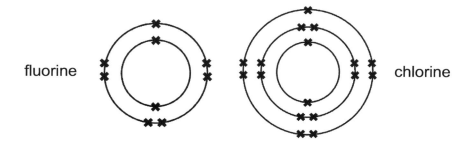

fluorine

chlorine

shield   electron   harder   attracted   further

When group 7 elements react, they all gain one_____ into their outer energy level.

Moving down group 7, it becomes_____to gain an electron. This is because the

outer energy level is_____ from the nucleus. Internal energy levels also

_____the outer energy level from the nucleus. For both of these reasons, the

electrons in the outer energy level are less _____to the nucleus. This makes it

harder for the outer energy level to gain an electron as we move down group 7.

Exam tip: Remember that a more reactive halogen can displace (push out)
a less reactive halogen from an aqueous solution of its salt.

2. Predict the products of the following reactions and explain your answer.

lithium iodide   +   chlorine ⟶

Explanation

sodium chloride   +   bromine ⟶

Explanation

Exam tip: remember that
the halogens get less
reactive down group 7.

Transition Elements

1. The periodic table is shown below.

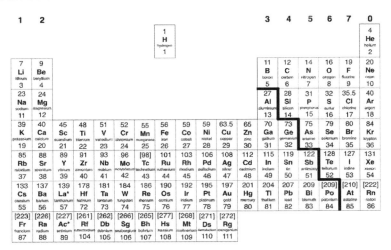

a. Whereabouts on the periodic table do we find the transition elements?

b. Transition elements are (circle the correct answer).

All metals	All non-metals	Both metals and non-metals

c. Complete the table to compare transition elements with the group 1 elements.

Group 1 elements	Transition elements
• Are soft	•
• Have low melting points	•
• Have a low density	•
• React very rapidly with oxygen, chlorine and water	•
• Form +1 ions eg Na⁺	•

d. How can we tell by looking at a compound whether it contains a transition element?

e. How are transition elements useful in chemical reactions?

Chapter 2: Structure and Bonding

• Describe the arrangement of particles in solids, liquids and gases.
• Describe what takes place during melting, freezing, boiling and condensation.
• Predict the state of substances at different temperatures based on given data.
• Describe the limitations of the simple particle model.
• Draw dot and cross diagrams for ionic compounds formed by metals in groups 1 and 2 with non metals in groups 6 and 7.
• Describe how ionic compounds form giant ionic lattices and use this to explain the properties of ionic compounds.
• Draw dot and cross diagrams and stick diagrams for the small covalent molecules hydrogen, chlorine, oxygen, nitrogen, hydrogen chloride, water, ammonia and methane.
• Describe and explain the properties of small covalent molecules.
• Describe the structure and properties of the giant covalent molecules diamond, silicon dioxide and graphite.
• Describe the structure and properties of graphene and fullerenes.
• Describe the bonding in polymer molecules including drawing the repeating unit for a given monomer.
• Describe the bonding in metals and use this to explain the properties of metals.
• Explain why alloys are harder than pure metals.
• Describe what is meant by PM10, PM2.5 and nanoparticles.
• Calculate the surface area:volume ratio and describe how this explains the properties of nanoparticles.
• Describe the limitations of bonding diagrams.

The Three States of Matter

1. The diagram below shows the particles in solids, liquids and gases.

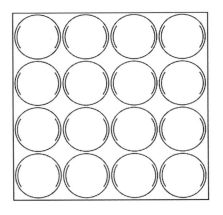
solid

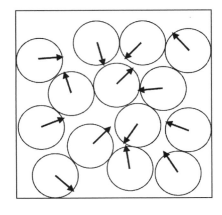
liquid

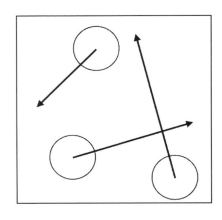
gas

Complete the table showing the properties of solids, liquids and gases.

In each case, you should explain the property by describing the particles.

State of matter	Can be compressed?	Flows and takes shape of container?
Solid	Yes / No	Yes / No
Liquid	Yes / No	Yes / No
Gas	Yes / No	Yes / No

2. When we melt a solid, we change it to a liquid.

This is shown in the diagram below.

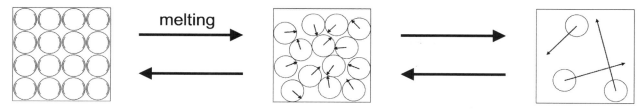

melting

a. Complete the diagram by writing the names of the processes taking place (melting has been done for you).

b. Looking at the diagram, how can we tell that particles in a liquid have more energy than the particles in a solid?

c. When we melt a solid, we need to put energy in.

What is this energy needed for?

d. The melting and boiling points of three compounds are shown in the table.

Compound	Melting point (°C)	Boiling point (°C)
sulfur dioxide	-72	-10
water	0	100
aluminium oxide	2072	2977

Which compound will be a gas at room temperature (20°C)?

Explain your answer.

e. Use the idea of forces between particles to explain why water has a lower melting point than aluminium oxide.

f. Which of the compounds above has the weakest forces between the particles?

Explain your answer.

g. State three limitations of the simple particle model of solids, liquids and gases.

Ionic Bonding

Exam tip: Ionic bonding happens when a metal reacts with a non-metal. We've already seen this in the sections on group 1 and group 7 in the last chapter.

1. Explain in terms of electrons why elements react.

2. Explain why the elements in group 0 (noble gases) do not react.

3. The reaction between lithium (group 1) and fluorine (group 7) is shown below.

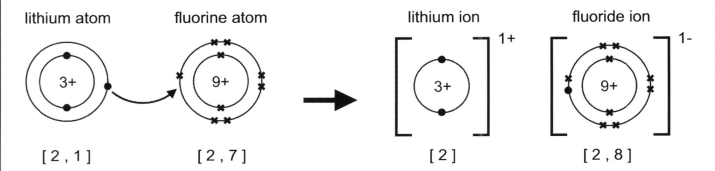

lithium atom	fluorine atom	lithium ion	fluoride ion
[2 , 1]	[2 , 7]	[2]	[2 , 8]

a. Describe in terms of electrons what happens when a lithium atom reacts with a fluorine atom.

b. Explain why the lithium and fluorine atoms are uncharged before they react.

c. Explain in terms of protons and electrons why the lithium ion has a 1 positive charge.

d. Explain in terms of protons and electrons why the fluoride ion has a 1 negative charge.

4. The reaction between sodium (group 1) and chlorine (group 7) is shown below.

a. Complete the diagram to show what happens when a sodium atom reacts with a chlorine atom.

You will need to draw the electronic structures of the ions produced and their charges.

| sodium atom | chlorine atom | sodium ion | chloride ion |

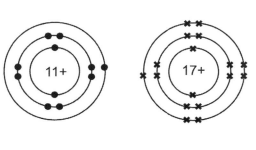 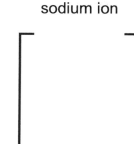 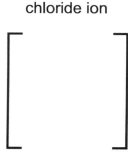

[2 , 8 , 1]   [2 , 8 , 7]   [   ]   [   ]

b. Describe what is happening in this reaction.

---

5. The reaction between potassium (group 1) and fluorine (group 7) is shown below.

Only outer electrons have been shown.

Complete the diagram to show the ions produced.

 +  →

[2 , 8 , 8 , 1]   [2 , 7]

---

6. Complete the paragraph using the words below.

loses   noble   ionic   +1   gains   full   -1

When a group 1 and a group 7 element react, _____ bonding takes place. The group

1 element _____ one electron to form an ion with a charge of _____ .

The group 7 element_____ one electron to form an ion with a charge of _____ .

Both ions have a _____ outer energy level just like_____ gases.

Ionic Bonding 2

1. Just like group 1, elements in group 2 carry out ionic bonding.

a. What happens when group 2 elements react?

Circle the correct answer.

> They gain
> 2 electrons

> They lose
> 2 electrons

> They share
> 2 electrons

b. Which type of ion is formed when group 2 elements react?

Circle the correct answer.

> Ions with a
> 2- charge

> Ions with a
> 2+ charge

> Ions with a
> 1+ charge

2. The reaction between magnesium (group 2) and oxygen (group 6) is shown below.

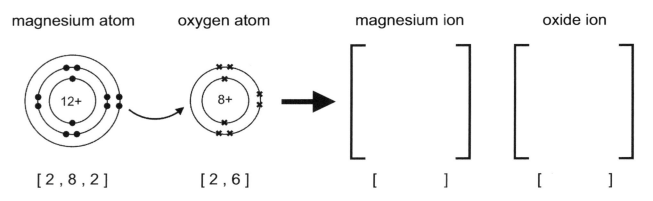

magnesium atom   oxygen atom   magnesium ion   oxide ion

[2 , 8 , 2]   [2 , 6]   [   ]   [   ]

a. Complete the diagram to show the ions produced in the reaction.

You should show the electronic structures and the charges on the ions.

b. Explain in terms of protons and electrons why the magnesium ion has a 2 positive charge.

c. Explain in terms of protons and electrons why the oxide ion has a 2 negative charge.

d. State which noble gas has the same electronic structure as both the magnesium ion and the oxide ion.

3. The reaction between calcium (group 2) and chlorine (group 7) is shown below.

Only the electrons in the outer energy levels are shown.

$$\text{Ca} \overset{\bullet}{\bullet} \quad + \quad 2 \underset{\times\times}{\overset{\times\times}{\times \text{Cl} \overset{\times}{\times}}} \longrightarrow$$

[2 , 8 , 8 , 2]   [2 , 8 , 7]

a. Complete the diagram to show the ions formed.

You should show the electronic structures and charges of the ions.

b. Explain in terms of electrons why the formula of calcium chloride is CaCl$_2$.

c. State which noble gas has the same electronic structure as both the calcium ion and the chloride ion.

---

4. The reaction between sodium (group 1) and oxygen (group 6) is shown below.

Only the electrons in the outer energy levels are shown.

$$2\,\text{Na} \bullet \quad + \quad \underset{\times\times}{\overset{\times\times}{\text{O} \overset{\times}{\underset{\times}{}}}} \longrightarrow$$

[2 , 8 , 1]   [2 , 6]

a. Complete the diagram to show the ions formed.

You should show the electronic structures and charges of the ions.

b. State the formula of sodium oxide.

Explain your answer in terms of electrons transferred.

c. State which noble gas has the same electronic structure as both the sodium ion and the oxide ion.

5. The diagrams below show a number of different ions.

In each case, identify the element involved and explain your answer (the first has been done for you).

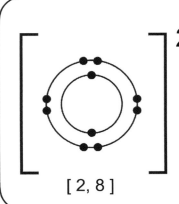

[2, 8]

Element = magnesium

There are ten electrons. The charge of 2+ tells us that two electrons must have been lost from the original element so the original element must have had twelve electrons. From the periodic table, we can see that magnesium has twelve electrons.

a. Element =

Explanation

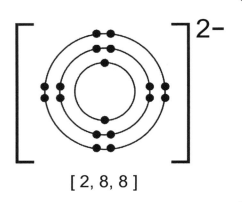

[2, 8, 8]

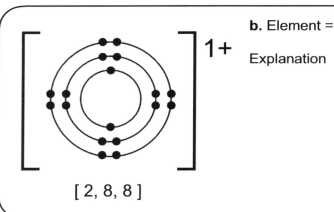

[2, 8, 8]

b. Element =

Explanation

c. Element =

Explanation

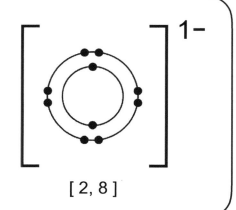

[2, 8]

Properties of Ionic Compounds

1. Potassium chloride is an ionic compound containing K^+ and Cl^- ions.

The diagrams show two different ways to represent the structure of ionic compounds.

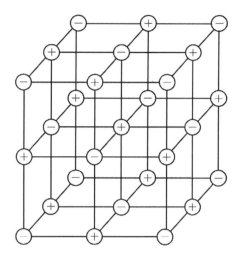

Ball and stick model   Space filling model

a. Label the potassium and chloride ions in the two diagrams.

b. Label the electrostatic forces of attraction in the ball and stick model.

c. What do scientists call a regular arrangement of positive and negative ions in 3 dimensions?

d. Draw lines to show one advantage and one disadvantage of each type of diagram.

The sizes of each ion are not shown correctly

Electrostatic forces are not shown

Ball and Stick Model

Space filling Model

The sizes of each ion are shown correctly

The electrostatic forces are shown

2. Two of the key properties of ionic compounds are their very high melting points and boiling points.

a. Describe what happens to the particles when we heat an ionic solid.

b. Explain why ionic solids have very high melting points.

c. The melting points of two ionic compounds are shown in the table.

Ionic compound	Ions present	Melting point (°C)
Sodium chloride	Na^+ Cl^-	801
Magnesium oxide	Mg^{2+} O^{2-}	2852

Suggest why the melting point of magnesium oxide is much greater than the melting point of sodium chloride. You should consider the charges on the ions and the strength of the electrostatic forces of attraction.

3. Another key property of ionic compounds is how they conduct electricity.

a. Explain why ionic compounds cannot conduct electricity when they are solids.

b. Ionic compounds can conduct electricity when they are melted or dissolved in water.

Explain why.

Covalent Bonding 1

1. Identify which of the following statements are true and which are false.

Then rewrite the false statements so that they are correct.

a. When a metal reacts with a non-metal, covalent bonding takes place.

b. In covalent bonding, a pair of electrons is shared between two atoms.

c. During covalent bonding, the atoms become a noble gas.

2. The diagram below shows the reaction between two hydrogen atoms to form a hydrogen molecule.

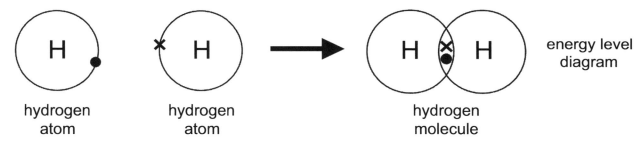

| hydrogen atom | hydrogen atom | hydrogen molecule | energy level diagram |

a. Label the covalent bond on the diagram above.

b. Describe in terms of electrons what is taking place during this reaction.

c. Complete the dot-cross diagram and stick diagrams for the hydrogen molecule.

dot-cross diagram   stick diagram

3. In covalent bonding, we only show the outer energy levels of the atoms involved.

Explain why we do not show the other energy levels.

4. The non-metal element chlorine is in group 7.

Atoms of chlorine have 7 electrons in their outer energy level.

a. Complete the outer energy-level diagram below to show the covalent bonding in a chlorine molecule Cl_2.

Use dots and crosses to show electrons.

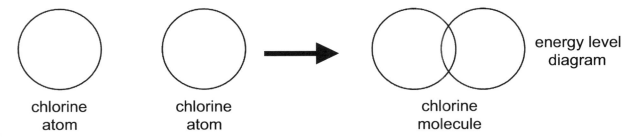

| chlorine atom | chlorine atom | chlorine molecule | energy level diagram |

b. Label the covalent bond on the diagram above.

c. Complete the dot-cross and stick diagrams to show the covalent bonding in a chlorine molecule Cl_2.

Remember that you only need to show the outer electrons.

Cl Cl   Cl Cl

dot-cross   stick
diagram   diagram

5. Hydrogen and chlorine can react to form hydrogen chloride.

a. Complete the energy level diagram below to show the covalent bonding in a hydrogen chloride molecule HCl.

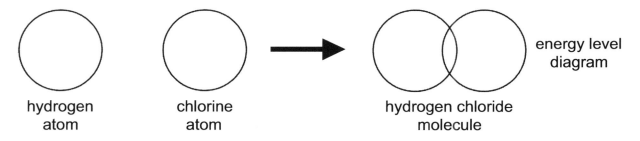

hydrogen atom   chlorine atom   hydrogen chloride molecule   energy level diagram

b. Label the covalent bond on the diagram above.

c. Complete the dot-cross and stick diagrams to show the covalent bonding in a hydrogen chloride molecule HCl.

Remember that you only need to show the outer electrons.

H Cl   H Cl

dot-cross   stick
diagram   diagram

Covalent Bonding 2

1. Water has the chemical formula H_2O.

a. Hydrogen atoms have one electron and oxygen atoms have six electrons in their outer energy level.

Complete the diagram below to show the covalent bonding in water. Only outer energy levels have been shown.

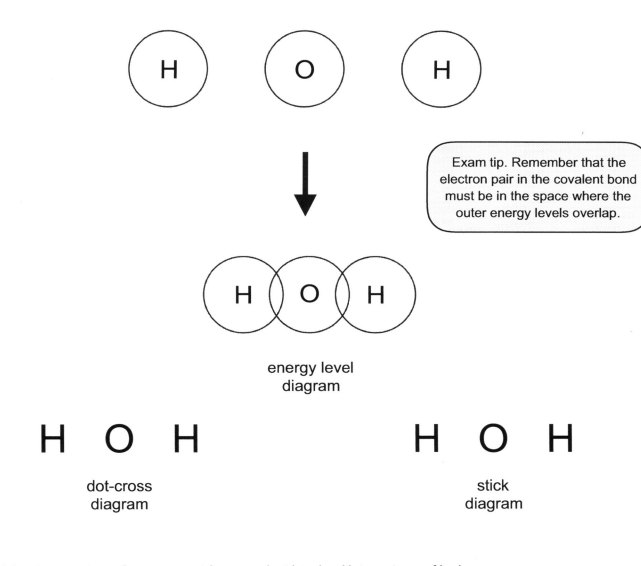

Exam tip. Remember that the electron pair in the covalent bond must be in the space where the outer energy levels overlap.

energy level
diagram

dot-cross
diagram

stick
diagram

b. Explain why one atom of oxygen must form covalent bonds with two atoms of hydrogen.

2. Ammonia has the chemical formula NH_3.

a. Hydrogen atoms have one electron and nitrogen atoms have five electrons in their outer energy level.

Complete the diagram below to show the covalent bonding in ammonia.

Only outer energy levels have been shown.

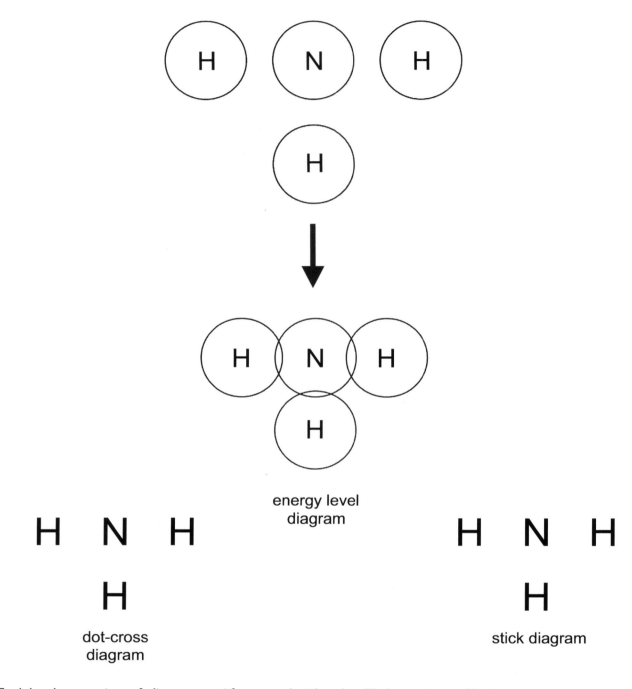

energy level
diagram

H N H
H

dot-cross
diagram

H N H
H

stick diagram

b. Explain why one atom of nitrogen must form covalent bonds with three atoms of hydrogen.

3. Methane has the chemical formula CH_4.

a. Hydrogen atoms have one electron and carbon atoms have four electrons in their outer energy level.

Complete the diagram below to show the covalent bonding in methane.

Only outer energy levels have been shown.

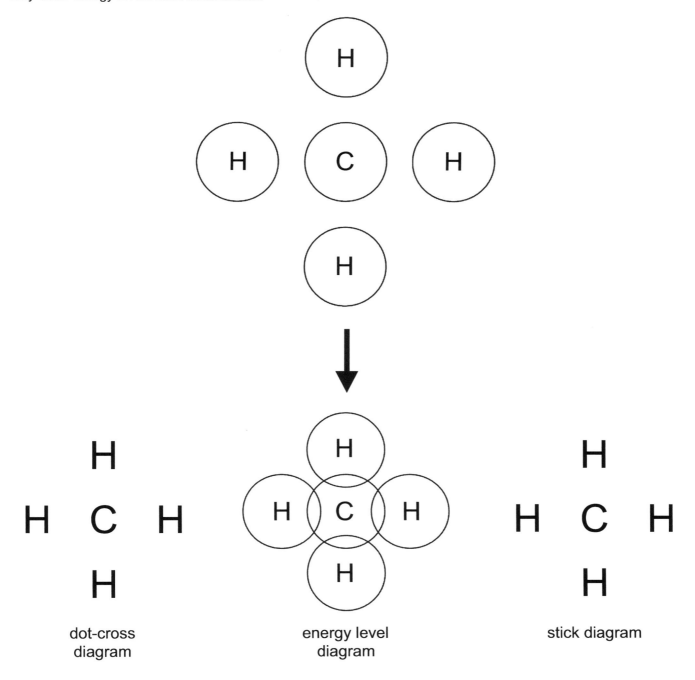

dot-cross
diagram

energy level
diagram

stick diagram

b. Explain why one atom of carbon must form covalent bonds with four atoms of hydrogen.

Covalent Bonding 3

All of the molecules that we have seen so far have single covalent bonds.
However, some molecules contain double or triple covalent bonds.

1. Oxygen molecules have the formula O_2.

a. Complete the diagrams to show the covalent bonding in a molecule of oxygen.

Only outer energy levels have been shown.

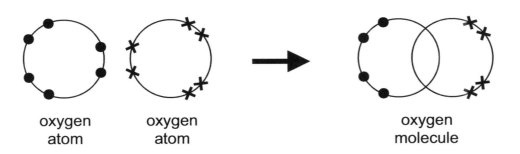

oxygen   oxygen   oxygen
atom   atom   molecule

O O
dot-cross
diagram

O O
stick diagram

b. On the energy level diagram, label the double covalent bond.

c. Explain how both atoms now have a full outer energy level.

2. Nitrogen molecules have the formula N_2.

a. Complete the diagrams to show the covalent bonding in a molecule of nitrogen.

Only outer energy levels have been shown.

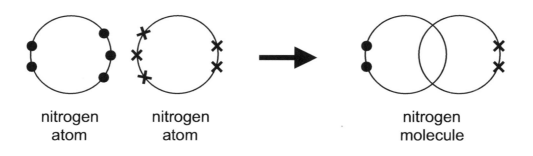

nitrogen   nitrogen   nitrogen
atom   atom   molecule

N N
dot-cross
diagram

N N
stick diagram

b. On the energy level diagram, label the triple covalent bond.

c. Explain how both atoms now have a full outer energy level.

Properties of Small Covalent Molecules

Exam tip: You need to be really clear on the properties of small covalent molecules. These include their melting and boiling points and whether they conduct electricity.

1. Small covalent molecules have low melting points and boiling points.

a. Select the correct word to complete the sentence below.

Small covalent molecules are usually
> gases
> liquids
> solids

at room temperature.

b. The diagram shows the small covalent molecule Cl_2 as a liquid and as a gas.

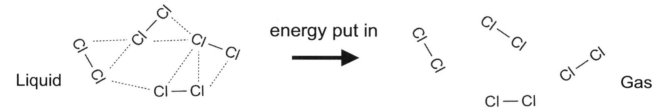

On the diagram, label the covalent bonds and the intermolecular forces.

c. Which process is shown in the diagram?

> melting

> boiling

> condensation

d. Explain why small covalent molecules have low melting and boiling points.

e. As the size of the covalent molecule increases, the melting and boiling points increase.

This is because the strength of the intermolecular forces... (select the correct box)

> decreases

> stays the same

> increases

2. Explain why small covalent molecules cannot conduct electricity.

Diamond and Silicon Dioxide

1. Giant covalent molecules have very different properties to small covalent molecules.

Which of the properties below apply to giant covalent molecules?

Contain only a small number of covalent bonds

Have high melting and boiling points

Are always solids at room temperature

Includes oxygen and methane

Have millions of strong covalent bonds

Are usually gases at room temperature

2. The diagram shows a tiny part of a diamond molecule.

a. Describe the bonding in the diamond molecule.

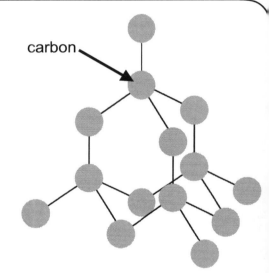

carbon

b. Explain why the melting point of diamond is greater than 3700°C.

c. Diamond cannot conduct electricity.

Explain why not.

3. The diagram below shows the structure of the giant covalent molecule silica.

Silica is also called silicon dioxide.

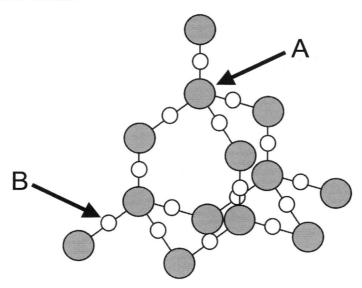

a. Which two elements are present in silicon dioxide?

| carbon | oxygen | silicon | chlorine |

b. Which of the elements are **A** and **B** in the diagram above?

A =

B =

c. The structure of silicon dioxide is similar to and different from the structure of diamond.

Describe how.

d. The melting point of silicon dioxide is over 1700ºC.

Use the structure to explain why the melting point is so high.

e. Suggest why silicon dioxide cannot conduct electricity.

Graphite

1. The diagram shows the structures of diamond and graphite.

Diamond

Graphite
(not to same scale)

a. Describe one similarity and one difference between the structure of graphite and the structure of diamond.

Similarity:

Difference:

b. Label the carbon atoms and covalent bonds on the diagram of graphite.

c. In graphite, the carbon atoms are arranged in hexagonal rings.
What does this mean?

2. Graphite has a melting point of around 4000°C.

a. Which of the following best explains why graphite has such a high melting point?

> **A.** There are weak intermolecular forces between the atoms

> **B.** There are no covalent bonds between the layers

> **C.** Graphite has millions of covalent bonds which take a lot of energy to break

b. Explain why the other two explanations are not correct.

3. The diagram below shows what happens when a force is applied to the layers in graphite.

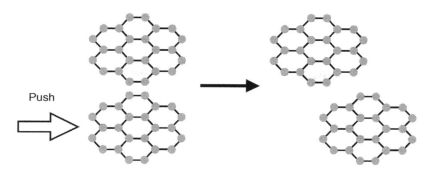

Push

Graphite feels slippery to touch.

Use the diagram above to explain why.

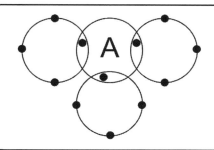

4. The diagram shows four carbon atoms in graphite.

a. Complete the diagram using crosses to show the electrons in the outer energy level of atom A.

Remember that carbon atoms have four electrons in their outer energy level.

b. Label the electron on atom A which is not in a covalent bond.

5. Graphite is an excellent conductor of both heat and electricity.

This is because it has delocalised electrons.

a. Explain what is meant by "delocalised electrons".

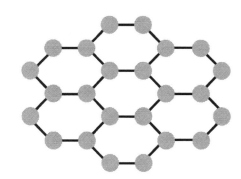

e^- e^- e^- e^- e^-
e^- e^-

b. Delocalised electrons allow graphite to conduct both heat and electricity.

Explain how.

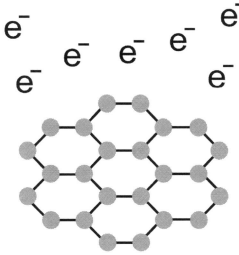

Graphene and Fullerenes

1. The diagram shows the structure of graphene.

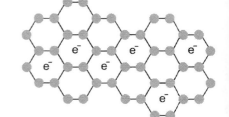

a. Use the diagram to describe the structure.

b. Explain why graphene is an excellent conductor of electricity.

c. What other property of graphene will make it useful for new materials?

2. The diagram below shows two examples of molecules called fullerenes.

Complete the paragraph using the words below.

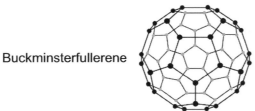

Buckminsterfullerene

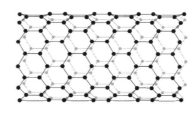

carbon nanotube

five   hollow   lubricant   hexagonal   seven

Fullerenes are molecules of carbon atoms with _____ shapes. Usually the carbon

atoms in fullerenes are arranged in _____ rings for example in carbon nanotubes.

However, Buckminsterfullerene also has rings containing _____ carbon atoms.

Other fullerenes can have rings of _____ carbon atoms. Buckminsterfullerene is

useful as a _____ , as catalysts and for delivering pharmaceuticals.

3. Carbon nanotubes have high tensile strength which makes them very useful.

a. What is meant by "high tensile strength"?

b. State a use of carbon nanotubes.

Bonding in Polymers

1. Complete the sentences by selecting the correct word in each box.

Polymer molecules are long
| chains |
| rings |
| balls |
formed by joining together thousands of monomers.

The monomers joined together to make a polymer are called
| alkanes. |
| catalysts. |
| alkenes. |

The polymer
| poly(ethane) |
| poly(ethene) |
| poly(propene) |
is made from the monomer ethene.

2. The diagram below shows four molecules of the monomer ethene.

a. Draw a diagram of the polymer produced from these monomers.

monomer = ethene

```
H    H    H    H    H    H    H    H
|    |    |    |    |    |    |    |
C == C    C == C    C == C    C == C
|    |    |    |    |    |    |    |
H    H    H    H    H    H    H    H
```

> Exam tip. The carbon atoms on the ends of the polymer you draw will not have enough hydrogen atoms. You do not need to worry about this for GCSE.

polymer = ...

b. Describe how the bonding between the carbon atoms is different in the monomer compared to the polymer?

3. The repeating unit for poly(ethene) is shown below.

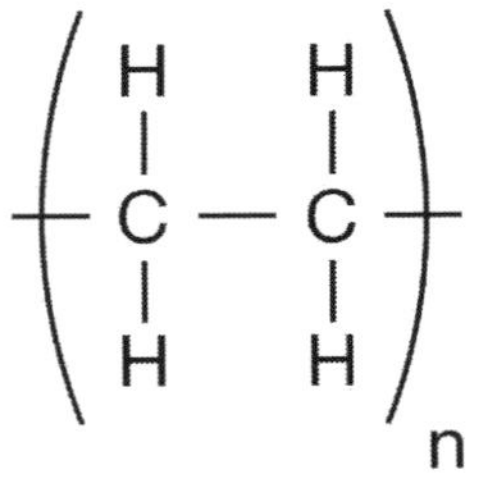

Describe three key features of any repeating unit.

-
-
-

4. Draw the repeating units for the polymers produced from the following monomers.

monomer =
chloroethene

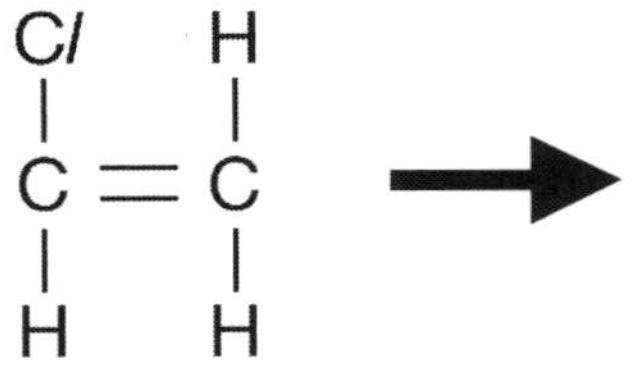

⟶

polymer =
(poly)chloroethene

monomer =
propene

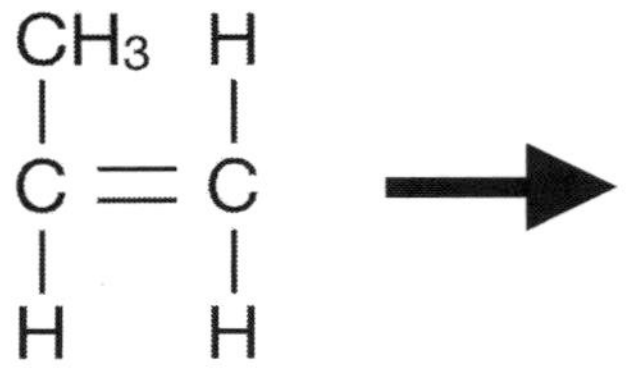

⟶

polymer =
(poly)propene

5. The diagram below shows the bonding between polymer molecules.

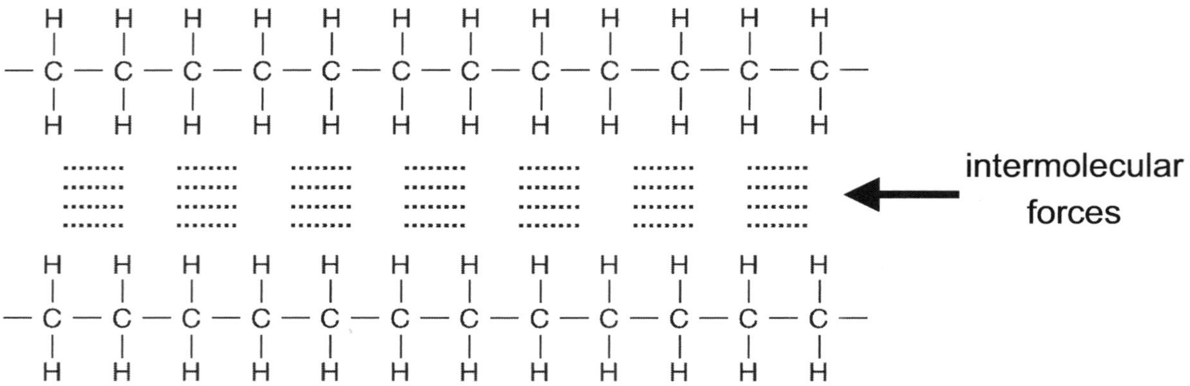

intermolecular forces

Use the diagram to explain why most polymers are solids at room temperature.

Metals and Alloys

1. The diagram shows how the atoms are arranged in a pure metal.

Describe the structure of metals using the words below.

giant structure　　　　**layers**　　　　**delocalised**

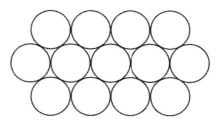

2. In metals, the electrons in the outer energy level are delocalised.

a. What is meant by the word "delocalised"?

b. The diagram below shows the atoms in the metal beryllium.

Complete the diagram to show how the electrons delocalise.

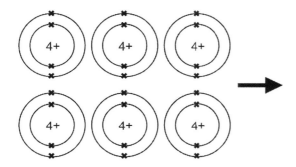

c. Once the electrons are delocalised, the atoms are described as positive ions.

Explain why in terms of the numbers of protons and electrons.

Exam tip: Remember that metallic bonding is the electrostatic attraction between the metal ions and the delocalised electrons.

---

3. What is meant by electrostatic attraction?

4. Explain why metals have high melting and boiling points.

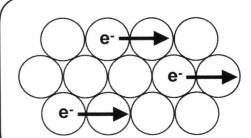

5. Use the diagram to explain why metals are good conductors of both heat and electricity.

Exam tip: Why are alloys harder than pure metals? It's all about how the atoms are arranged. Make sure to learn the details.

6. The diagram below shows the atoms in a pure metal such as iron and an alloy such as steel.

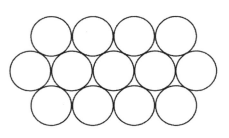

pure metal

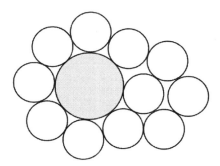

alloy

a. Explain why pure metals can be bent and shaped.

b. What is meant by an alloy?

c. Explain why alloys are harder than pure metals.

Nanoparticles

1. Link the words on the left to the correct name in the centre and the size on the right.

1 mm	1 nanometre	1×10^{-6} metre
1 μm	1 millimetre	1×10^{-9} metre
1 nm	1 micrometre	1×10^{-3} metre

2. Arrange the following sizes on the scale from smallest to largest.

5×10^{-6} m	4 nm	0.5 mm	4.2×10^{-9} m	6 μm

smallest ———————————————————————————————➤ largest

3. The particulate matter (or PM) number gives us information on the sizes of particles.

The number tells us the maximum size of that particle in micrometres.

a. Fill in the spaces on the following different particle sizes.

PM 10	PM 2.5	PM _____
Also called coarse particles or dust	Also called fine particles	Also called nanoparticles
Size range =	Size range =	Size range =
10 μm to _____ μm	2.5 μm to _____ μm	0.1 μm to _____ nm
Contain _____ thousands of atoms	Contain _____ thousands of atoms	Contain a few _____ atoms

b. What do you think the PM number for nanoparticles would be?

Explain your answer.

4. The surface area : volume ratio tells us the amount of surface area for a given volume.

a. Calculate the surface area : volume ratios of the two particles below.

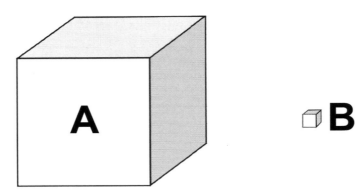

Particle	Length of each side (μm)	Surface area (μm^2)	Volume (μm^3)	Surface area: volume ratio
A	10			
B	1			

b. Describe what happens to the surface area : volume ratio of the particles as we decrease the size of the particle by 10 times.

Exam tip: Nanoparticles are tiny so even a small mass of nanoparticles has a huge surface area. This means that we only need to use a small amount for a given function.

5. Nanoparticles are used in lots of different products.

a. State three uses of nanoparticles.

b. Some scientists recommend that we are cautious when using nanoparticles for products such as suncreams and deodorants.

Explain why.

Limitations of Bonding Diagrams

Exam tip: Each type of bonding diagram has limitations. They are really worth making an effort to learn as they are likely to be asked in the exam.

1. The dot and cross diagram and the 2 dimensional stick diagram for methane are shown below.

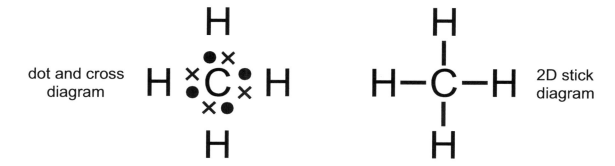

dot and cross diagram

2D stick diagram

a. Describe one advantage and one disadvantage of dot and cross diagrams.

Advantage:

Disadvantage:

b. Describe the disadvantages of a 2 dimensional stick diagram such as the one above.

2. The diagram shows the 3-dimensional stick diagram for methane.

Describe the advantage of a 3-dimensional stick diagram compared to a 2 dimensional stick diagram.

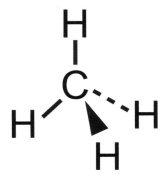

3. Diagrams to show ionic compounds also have advantages and disadvantages.

a. The "ball and stick" and "space-filling" diagrams for an ionic compound are shown below.

Complete the boxes to show one advantage and one disadvantage of each diagram.

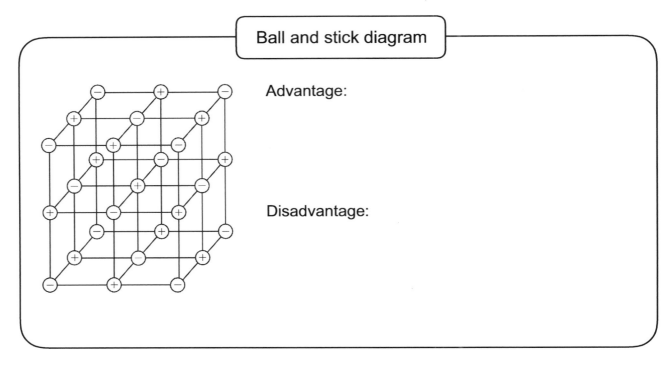

Ball and stick diagram

Advantage:

Disadvantage:

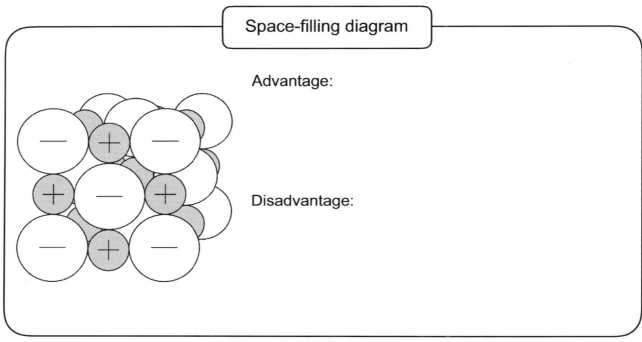

Space-filling diagram

Advantage:

Disadvantage:

b. Describe one disadvantage shared by both ball and stick and space-filling diagrams.

Chapter 3: Quantitative Chemistry

• Describe what is meant by the conservation of mass.
• Use the idea of conservation of mass to calculate the masses of reactants or products in a chemical reaction.
• Use the periodic table to determine the charges on metal and non-metal ions.
• Determine the formula of ionic compounds using charges provided.
• Balance simple chemical equations.
• State what is meant by relative formula mass and determine the relative formula mass for different molecules.
• Calculate the number of moles of an element.
• Calculate the number of moles of a compound.
• Calculate the mass of a number of moles.
• Use moles to balance complex chemical equations.
• Use Avogadro's constant to calculate the number of atoms, molecules, ions and electrons.
• Use reacting mass calculations to calculate the mass of reactants or products in chemical reactions.
• State what is meant by the limiting reactant and determine the limiting reactant for a chemical reaction.
• Calculate the concentration of solutions in g / dm^3.
• Calculate the percentage yield for a given reaction.
• Calculate atom economy.
• Calculate the concentration of solutions in mol / dm^3 and use these to calculate the mass or number of moles of reactants or products in a chemical reaction.
• Calculate volumes of gases used or produced in chemical reactions.

Conservation of Mass

1. The equation below shows the neutralisation reaction between hydrochloric acid and the alkali sodium hydroxide.

| hydrochloric acid | + | sodium hydroxide | $\longrightarrow$ | sodium chloride | + | water |

$$HCl_{(aq)} + NaOH_{(aq)} \longrightarrow NaCl_{(aq)} + H_2O_{(l)}$$

a. Which chemicals are the reactants in this reaction?

b. Which chemicals are the products?

c. A scientist reacted 73 g of hydrochloric acid with 80 g of sodium hydroxide.
Calculate the total mass of reactants used.

d. Using the law of conservation of mass, state the total mass of products that must be made in this reaction.

e. In this reaction, the scientist made a total of 117 g of sodium chloride.
Calculate the mass of water that they also made.

f. Explain how this reaction has obeyed the law of conservation of mass.

2. The equation below shows the reaction between sulfuric acid and the metal lithium.

sulfuric acid $\quad+\quad$ lithium $\quad\longrightarrow\quad$ lithium sulfate $\quad+\quad$ hydrogen

$$H_2SO_{4\,(aq)} \quad+\quad 2Li_{(s)} \quad\longrightarrow\quad Li_2SO_{4\,(aq)} \quad+\quad H_{2\,(g)}$$

a. A scientist carried out this reaction and produced 110 g of lithium sulfate and 2 g of hydrogen.
Calculate the total mass of product.

b. Using the law of conservation of mass, state the total mass of reactants used.

c. In this reaction, the scientist used 98 g of sulfuric acid.
Calculate the mass of lithium that the scientist used.

3. Calcium carbonate breaks down when heated.

calcium carbonate $\quad\xrightarrow{\text{heat}}\quad$ calcium oxide $\quad+\quad$ carbon dioxide

$$CaCO_{3\,(s)} \quad\longrightarrow\quad CaO_{(s)} \quad+\quad CO_{2\,(g)}$$

a. A scientist reacted 200 g of calcium carbonate and produced 112g of calcium oxide.
Calculate the mass of carbon dioxide produced.

b. The scientist found that the mass of carbon dioxide was less than expected.
Suggest a reason why this may have happened.

Charges on Ions

1. Ions are often formed during chemical reactions.

a. Which of these is the correct definition of an ion?

| An atom which is sharing electrons with another atom | An atom which has more neutrons than protons | An atom which has an overall charge |

b. Complete the sentences below.

Metal atoms always form ions with a _____ charge.

Non-metal atoms usually form ions with a _____ charge.

c. Use the periodic table to determine the charges on the following metal ions.

In each case, explain your answer.

| K | Sr | B |

2. Chromium and nickel are both transition metals.

a. Why can we not easily determine the charge on ions such as chromium or nickel.

b. Vanadium is also a transition metal. In some compounds, vanadium is written as vanadium (III).

What is meant by this?

3. Use the periodic table to determine the charges on the following non-metal ions.

In each case, explain your answer.

| Se | I |

Formula of Ionic Compounds

1. The calcium ion and chloride ion are shown on the right.

The ionic compound calcium chloride has the formula $CaCl_2$.

Explain why calcium chloride has no overall charge.

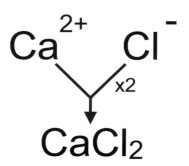

2. The table shows some common ions.

Use the table of ions to work out the formulas of the following ionic compounds.

lithium	Li^+
sodium	Na^+
magnesium	Mg^{2+}
calcium	Ca^{2+}
aluminium	Al^{3+}
ammonium	NH_4^+
chloride	Cl^-
iodide	I^-
nitrate	NO_3^-
oxide	O^{2-}
carbonate	CO_3^{2-}
sulfate	SO_4^{2-}
phosphate	PO_4^{3-}

magnesium iodide

lithium oxide

calcium carbonate

aluminium chloride

ammonium nitrate

sodium phosphate

3. The following formulas are all wrong.

Write the correct formulas in the spaces below.

magnesium oxide = Mg_2O Correct answer =

lithium chloride = $LiCl_2$ Correct answer =

aluminium oxide = Al_2O_2 Correct answer =

4. Write the formulas of the following compounds.

All of the formulas require brackets.

calcium nitrate	ammonium carbonate	iron (II) phosphate

Balancing Chemical Equations

1. The formula of magnesium sulfate is $MgSO_4$.

Using the periodic table, state the elements in magnesium sulfate and the number of atoms of each element.

2. Balance the following equations by counting the atoms on either side of the arrow.

$$Mg(OH)_2 \quad + \quad \underline{\quad} HCl \quad \longrightarrow \quad MgCl_2 \quad + \quad 2H_2O$$

$$N_2 \quad + \quad \underline{\quad} H_2 \quad \longrightarrow \quad 2NH_3$$

$$CuSO_4 \quad + \quad \underline{\quad} NaOH \quad \longrightarrow \quad Cu(OH)_2 \quad + \quad Na_2SO_4$$

$$CH_4 \quad + \quad \underline{\quad} O_2 \quad \longrightarrow \quad CO_2 \quad + \quad \underline{\quad} H_2O$$

Relative Formula Mass

1. What is the definition of relative formula mass (M_r)?

2. Calculate the relative formula masses of the following:

$MgCl_2$ (A_r Mg = 24, A_r Cl = 35.5)

K_2SO_4 (A_r K = 39, A_r S = 32, A_r O = 16)

$Ca(OH)_2$ (A_r Ca = 40, A_r O = 16, A_r H = 1)

$Al(NO_3)_3$ (A_r Al = 27, A_r N = 14, A_r O = 16)

3. The following relative formula masses are incorrect.

Explain why and state the correct M_r in each case.

Li_2SO_4 $M_r = 103g$ (A_r Li = 7, A_r S = 32, A_r O = 16)

$Ca(NO_3)_2$ $M_r = 204$ (A_r Ca = 40, A_r N = 14, A_r O = 16)

$2ZnCO_3$ $M_r = 250$ (A_r Zn = 65, A_r C = 12, A_r O = 16)

Calculating Moles of an Element

$$\text{number of moles of an element (n)} = \frac{\text{mass (m)}}{\text{relative atomic mass (A}_r\text{)}}$$

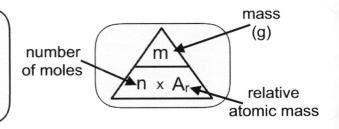

number of moles

mass (g)

relative atomic mass

1. Calculate the number of moles of these elements.

a. 64 g of sulfur (A_r S = 32)

b. 40.5 g of aluminium (A_r Al = 27)

c. 96 g of magnesium (A_r Mg = 24)

2. Calculate the number of moles of these elements.

State your answers to 3 significant figures.

a. 0.2 g of lithium (A_r Li = 7)

b. 6.3 g of potassium (A_r K = 39)

3. Calculate the number of moles of these elements.

State all your answers in standard form to the significant figures shown.

a. 4600 g of sodium (A_r Na = 23) 1 significant figure

b. 4995 g of beryllium (A_r Be = 9) 2 significant figures

c. 0.276 g of boron (A_r B = 11) 2 significant figures

Calculating Moles of a Compound

$$\text{number of moles of a compound (n)} = \frac{\text{mass (m)}}{\text{relative formula mass (}M_r\text{)}}$$

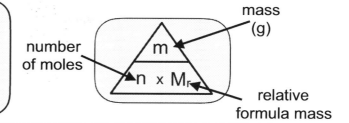

number of moles

mass (g)

relative formula mass

m

$n \times M_r$

---

1. 930 g of sodium oxide (Na_2O) are produced in a reaction.

a. Calculate the relative formula mass of sodium oxide. A_r Na = 23, A_r O = 16.

b. Calculate the number of moles of sodium oxide produced in the reaction.

---

2. A scientist needs 2540 g of lithium fluoride (LiF).

a. Calculate the relative formula mass of lithium fluoride. A_r Li = 7, A_r F = 19.

b. Calculate the number of moles of lithium fluoride that the scientist needs.

Give your answer to 3 significant figures.

---

3. A scientist needs 1457 g of zinc iodide (ZnI_2).

a. Calculate the relative formula mass of zinc iodide. Ar Zn = 65, Ar I = 127.

b. Calculate the number of moles of zinc iodide needed.

Give your answer to 3 significant figures.

Calculating the Mass of a Number of Moles

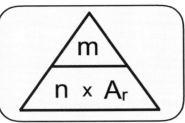

Exam tip: We can use the triangles to calculate the mass of a given number of moles.

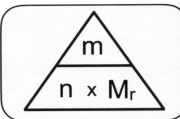

1. Calculate the mass in grams of the following number of moles.

a. 3 moles of calcium (A_r Ca = 40)

b. 5 moles of zinc (A_r Zn = 65)

2. Calculate the mass in grams of the following, to 3 significant figures.

a. 0.374 moles of iron (A_r Fe = 56)

b. 0.0173 moles of silicon (A_r Si = 28)

c. 9.33 moles of potassium (A_r K = 39)

3. Calculate the mass in grams of the following.

Give your answers in standard form to 3 significant figures.

a. 3.851 moles of aluminium (A_r Al = 27)

b. 12.63 moles of carbon (A_r C = 12)

c. 2.5×10^{-3} moles of boron (A_r B = 11)

4. A scientist needs 1.5 moles of the compound magnesium sulfide (MgS).

a. Calculate the relative formula mass of magnesium sulfide. A_r Mg = 24, A_r S = 32.

b. Calculate the mass in grams of magnesium sulfide that the scientist needs.

5. A scientist needs 3 moles of the compound lithium oxide (Li_2O).

a. Calculate the relative formula mass of lithium oxide. A_r Li = 7, A_r O = 16.

b. Calculate the mass in grams of lithium oxide that the scientist needs.

6. A scientist produces 7.3 moles of sodium sulfate (Na_2SO_4).

a. Calculate the relative formula mass of sodium sulfate. A_r Na = 23, A_r S = 32, A_r O = 16.

b. Calculate the mass in grams of sodium sulfate that the scientist makes.
Give your answer to 4 significant figures.

7. A fertiliser company makes 700 moles of ammonium nitrate (NH_4NO_3).

a. Calculate the relative formula mass of ammonium nitrate. A_r H = 1, A_r N = 14, A_r O = 16.

b. Calculate the mass in grams of ammonium nitrate that the company makes.
Give your answer in standard form.

Using Moles to Balance Equations

1. The reaction between iron (III) chloride and ammonium hydroxide is shown below.

iron (III) chloride		ammonium hydroxide		iron (III) hydroxide		ammonium chloride
$FeCl_3$	+	NH_4OH	$\longrightarrow$	$Fe(OH)_3$	+	NH_4Cl

In this reaction, 650 g of iron (III) chloride reacted with 420 g of ammonium hydroxide. 428 g of iron (III) hydroxide and 642 g of ammonium chloride were produced.

Use these numbers to balance the equation. A_r Fe = 56, A_r Cl = 35.5, A_r N = 14, A_r O = 16, A_r H = 1

2. The reaction between aluminium carbide and water is shown below.

aluminium carbide		water		aluminium hydroxide		methane
Al_4C_3	+	H_2O	$\longrightarrow$	$Al(OH)_3$	+	CH_4

In this reaction, 720 g of aluminium carbide reacted with 1080 g of water. 1560 g of aluminium hydroxide and 240 g of methane were produced.

Use these numbers to balance the equation. A_r Al = 27, A_r C = 12, Ar H = 1, Ar O = 16.

3. The reaction between potassium superoxide and carbon dioxide is shown below.

potassium superoxide		carbon dioxide		potassium carbonate		oxygen
KO_2	+	CO_2	$\longrightarrow$	K_2CO_3	+	O_2

In this reaction, 1420 g of potassium superoxide reacted with 440 g of carbon dioxide. 1380 g of potassium carbonate and 480 g of oxygen were produced.

Use these numbers to balance the equation. A_r K = 39, A_r O = 16, A_r C = 12

4. The reaction between cyclohexane and oxygen is shown below.

cyclohexane		oxygen		carbon dioxide		water
C_6H_{12}	+	O_2	$\longrightarrow$	CO_2	+	H_2O

In this reaction, 756 g of cyclohexane reacted with 2592 g of oxygen. 2376 g of carbon dioxide and 972 g of water were produced.

Use these numbers to balance the equation. A_r C = 12, A_r H = 1, A_r O = 16

Avogadro's Constant 1

1. Calculate the number of moles of atoms in one mole of the following substances.

a. K

b. Cl_2

c. MgO

d. Na_2O

e. H_2O_2

f. $Be(OH)_2$

2. Calculate the number of moles of atoms in the following.

a. 1 mole of lithium chloride $LiCl$.

b. 3 moles of beryllium fluoride BeF_2.

c. 4 moles of calcium carbonate $CaCO_3$.

d. 7 moles of magnesium nitrate $Mg(NO_3)_2$

3. Aluminium atoms form the aluminium ion as follows.

$$Al \longrightarrow Al^{3+} + 3 \text{ electrons}$$

a. How many moles of aluminium ions form when 4 moles of aluminium atoms react.

b. How many moles of electrons are lost when 4 moles of aluminium atoms react?

c. Explain your answer to b.

Avogadro's Constant 2

1. State the value of Avogadro's constant in standard form.

2. A sample of zinc chloride ($ZnCl_2$) has a mass of 136 g.

a. Calculate the relative formula mass (M_r) of zinc chloride. A_r Zn = 65, A_r Cl = 35.5

b. Calculate the number of moles of zinc chloride in the sample.

c. Calculate the number of moles of atoms in the sample.

d. Using Avogadro's constant, calculate the number of atoms in the sample.

3. Manganese atoms can lose electrons to form the manganese ion.

This is shown below.

$$Mn \longrightarrow Mn^{4+} + 4\ electrons$$

a. A sample of manganese has a mass of 220 g.

Calculate the number of moles of manganese ions that could be produced from this sample. A_r Mn = 55.

b. Using Avogadro's constant and your answer to **a**, calculate the number of manganese ions produced.

c. Calculate the number of electrons produced.

Reacting Masses 1

1. 80 g of calcium was reacted with unlimited iodine.

calcium   iodine   calcium iodide

Ca + I_2 $\longrightarrow$ CaI_2

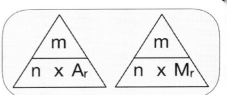

a. Calculate the number of moles of calcium that were used. A_r Ca = 40.

b. Using the large numbers in the chemical equation, state the number of moles of calcium iodide that could be produced.

c. Calculate the relative formula mass of calcium iodide. A_r Ca = 40, A_r I = 127.

d. Calculate the mass of calcium iodide made.

---

2. 612 g of barium oxide reacted with unlimited water to form barium hydroxide.

barium   water   barium
oxide   hydroxide

BaO + H_2O $\longrightarrow$ $Ba(OH)_2$

a. Calculate the number of moles of barium oxide used. Mr BaO = 153.

b. Using the large numbers in the chemical equation, state the number of moles of barium hydroxide that could be produced.

c. Calculate the relative formula mass of barium hydroxide. A_r Ba = 137, A_r O = 16, A_r H = 1.

d. Calculate the mass of barium hydroxide made.

3. When heated strongly, magnesium carbonate produced 176 g of carbon dioxide.

magnesium carbonate		magnesium oxide		carbon dioxide
$MgCO_3$	$\xrightarrow{\text{heat}}$	MgO	+	CO_2

a. Calculate the number of moles of carbon dioxide produced. M_r CO_2 = 44.

b. Using the large numbers in the chemical equation, state the number of moles of magnesium carbonate required to make this.

c. Calculate the relative formula mass of magnesium carbonate. A_r Mg = 24, A_r C = 12, A_r O = 16.

d. Calculate the mass of magnesium carbonate required for this reaction.

---

4. Sulfur trioxide and water reacted to produce 490 g of sulfuric acid.

sulfur trioxide		water		sulfuric acid
SO_3	+	H_2O	$\longrightarrow$	H_2SO_4

a. Calculate the number of moles of sulfuric acid produced. M_r H_2SO_4 = 98.

b. Using the large numbers in the chemical equation, state the number of moles of sulfur trioxide required to make this.

c. Calculate the relative formula mass of sulfur trioxide. A_r S = 32, A_r O = 16.

d. Calculate the mass of sulfur trioxide required for this reaction.

Reacting Masses 2

1. 188 g of potassium oxide was reacted with unlimited water.

potassium oxide		water		potassium hydroxide
K_2O	+	H_2O	$\longrightarrow$	2KOH

a. Calculate the number of moles of potassium oxide that were used. M_r K_2O = 94.

b. Using the large numbers in the chemical equation, state the number of moles of potassium hydroxide that could be produced.

c. Calculate the relative formula mass of potassium hydroxide. A_r K = 39, A_r O = 16, A_r H = 1.

d. Calculate the mass of potassium hydroxide made.

2. 252 g of nitric acid was reacted with unlimited beryllium hydroxide.

beryllium hydroxide		nitric acid		beryllium nitrate		water
$Be(OH)_2$	+	$2HNO_3$	$\longrightarrow$	$Be(NO_3)_2$	+	H_2O

a. Calculate the number of moles of nitric acid that were used. M_r HNO_3 = 63.

b. Using the large numbers in the chemical equation, state the number of moles of beryllium nitrate that could be produced.

c. Calculate the relative formula mass of beryllium nitrate. A_r Be = 9, A_r N = 14, A_r O = 16.

d. Calculate the mass of beryllium nitrate made.

3. In the following reaction, 272 g of zinc chloride were made.

| zinc | hydrochloric acid | zinc chloride | hydrogen |

$$Zn \quad + \quad \underline{}HCl \quad \longrightarrow \quad ZnCl_2 \quad + \quad H_2$$

a. Balance the equation by inserting a large number in the space provided.

b. Calculate how many moles of zinc chloride were made. M_r $ZnCl_2$ = 136.

c. Using the large numbers in the chemical equation, state the number of moles of hydrochloric acid needed for this reaction.

d. Calculate the relative formula mass of hydrochloric acid. A_r H = 1, A_r Cl = 35.5.

e. Calculate the mass of hydrochloric acid needed.

---

4. In the following reaction, 136 g of ammonia were made.

| nitrogen | hydrogen | ammonia |

$$N_2 \quad + \quad 3H_2 \quad \longrightarrow \quad \underline{}NH_3$$

a. Balance the equation by inserting a large number in the space provided.

b. Calculate how many moles of ammonia were made. M_r NH_3 = 17.

c. Using the large numbers in the chemical equation, state the number of moles of nitrogen needed for this reaction.

d. Calculate the mass of nitrogen needed. Mr N_2 = 28.

Limiting Reactant

1. Explain what is meant by the term "limiting reactant".

2. Identify the limiting reactant and the excess reactant in the reactions below.

a. 1 mole of calcium was reacted with 0.8 moles of bromine.

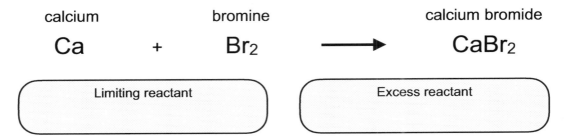

calcium		bromine		calcium bromide
Ca	+	Br_2	$\longrightarrow$	$CaBr_2$

Limiting reactant	Excess reactant

b. 2 moles of strontium oxide were reacted with 2.4 moles of sulfuric acid.

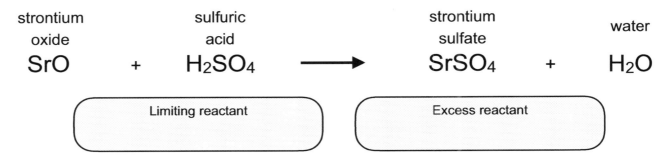

strontium oxide		sulfuric acid		strontium sulfate		water
SrO	+	H_2SO_4	$\longrightarrow$	$SrSO_4$	+	H_2O

Limiting reactant	Excess reactant

c. 0.1 moles of copper chloride were reacted with 0.15 moles of zinc.

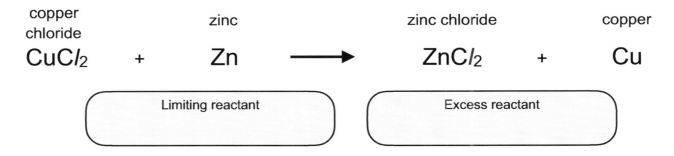

copper chloride		zinc		zinc chloride		copper
$CuCl_2$	+	Zn	$\longrightarrow$	$ZnCl_2$	+	Cu

Limiting reactant	Excess reactant

d. 6 moles of carbon dioxide reacted with 5.8 moles of water.

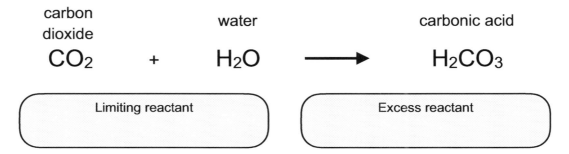

carbon dioxide		water		carbonic acid
CO_2	+	H_2O	$\longrightarrow$	H_2CO_3

Limiting reactant	Excess reactant

3. 1.3 moles of magnesium reacted with 1.2 moles of lead iodide.

magnesium		lead iodide		magnesium iodide		lead
Mg	+	PbI_2	$\longrightarrow$	MgI_2	+	Pb

a. State the limiting reactant in this reaction.

b. Using your answer to part a, state the number of moles of magnesium iodide produced in this reaction.

c. Calculate the relative formula mass of magnesium iodide. A_r Mg = 24, A_r I = 127.

d. Calculate the mass of magnesium iodide produced in this reaction.

4. 2.5 moles of hydrogen reacted with 3.5 moles of chlorine.

hydrogen		chlorine		hydrogen chloride
H_2	+	Cl_2	$\longrightarrow$	$2HCl$

a. State the limiting reactant in this reaction.

b. Determine the number of moles of chlorine that will take part in this reaction.

c. Calculate the relative formula mass of chlorine. A_r Cl = 35.5.

d. Calculate the mass of chlorine that will take part in this reaction.

Concentration of Solutions

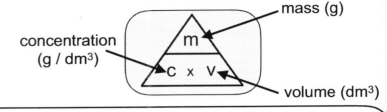

concentration
(g / dm³)

mass (g)

volume (dm³)

Exam tip: You need to learn this triangle.
Remember that the volume must be in dm³.

1. Complete the following paragraph using the words below.

water   **solution**   **solvent**   **mass**

A solute is a chemical dissolved in a _____ . In Chemistry, _____

is often used as a solvent. The concentration tells us the _____ of a solute

in a given volume of _____ .

2. Calculate the concentrations (in g / dm³) of the following solutions.

a. 200 g of lithium chloride in a final volume of
0.5 dm³ of water.

b. 0.5 g of copper sulfate in a final volume of
200 cm³ of water.

3. Calculate the volumes (in dm³) needed for the following solutions.

a. 150 g of sodium iodide at a final concentration of
75 g / dm³.

b. 64 g of zinc nitrate at a final concentration of
256 g / dm³.

4. Calculate the mass (in g) needed for the following solutions.

a. 2 dm³ of potassium carbonate at a final concentration
of 100 g / dm³.

b. 400 cm³ of silver nitrate at a final concentration of
100 g / dm³.

5. Circle the correct answers in the sentences below.

If we increase the mass of solute, then the concentration increases / decreases.

If we increase the volume of solution, then the concentration increases / decreases.

Calculating Percentage Yield

$$\% \text{ yield} = \frac{\text{mass of product actually made}}{\text{maximum theoretical mass of product}} \times 100$$

1. Calcium carbonate breaks down when heated.

The equation is shown below.

calcium carbonate	heat	calcium oxide		carbon dioxide
$CaCO_3$	$\longrightarrow$	CaO	+	CO_2

a. Calculate the relative formula mass of calcium carbonate. A_r Ca = 40, A_r C = 12, A_r O = 16.

b. 400 g of calcium carbonate was reacted.

Calculate the number of moles of calcium carbonate in the reaction.

c. Using the large numbers in the chemical equation, state the number of moles of calcium oxide that could be produced.

d. Calculate the relative formula mass of calcium oxide. A_r Ca = 40, A_r O = 16.

e. Calculate the total mass of calcium oxide that could be produced in this reaction.

f. In this reaction, 168 g of calcium oxide was produced.

Calculate the percentage yield of the reaction.

g. Suggest a reason why the percentage yield was less than 100%.

2. 48 g of magnesium was reacted with excess copper sulfate as shown below.

magnesium		copper sulfate		magnesium sulfate		copper
Mg	$+$	$CuSO_4$	$\longrightarrow$	$MgSO_4$	$+$	Cu

a. Calculate the number of moles of magnesium in the reaction. A_r Mg = 24.

b. Using the large numbers in the chemical equation, state the number of moles of copper that could be produced.

c. Calculate the total mass of copper that could be produced in this reaction. A_r Cu = 63.5.

d. In this reaction, 85 g of copper was produced.

Calculate the percentage yield of the reaction (state your answer to 2 significant figures).

e. A student calculated the percentage yield for this reaction at 149%.

Explain why the percentage yield for any reaction cannot be greater than 100%.

f. Describe the mistake that the student made in their calculation.

Calculating Percentage Yield 2

1. 135 g of lithium oxide was reacted with excess water as shown below.

lithium oxide		water		lithium hydroxide
Li_2O	+	H_2O	$\longrightarrow$	$2LiOH$

a. Calculate the relative formula mass of lithium oxide. A_r Li = 7, A_r O = 16.

b. Calculate the number of moles of lithium oxide in the reaction.

c. Using the large numbers in the chemical equation, state the number of moles of lithium hydroxide that could be produced.

d. Calculate the relative formula mass of lithium hydroxide. A_r Li = 7, A_r O = 16, A_r H = 1.

e. Calculate the mass of lithium hydroxide that could be produced in this reaction.

f. In this reaction, 54 g of lithium hydroxide was produced.

Calculate the percentage yield of the reaction.

g. The reaction was repeated but this time, the percentage yield increased to 35%.

Calculate the mass of lithium hydroxide produced in this reaction.

2. In the reaction below, 552 g of potassium carbonate was reacted with excess hydrochloric acid.

potassium carbonate		hydrochloric acid		potassium chloride		carbon dioxide		water
K_2CO_3	+	$2HCl$	$\longrightarrow$	$2KCl$	+	CO_2	+	H_2O

a. Calculate the relative formula mass of potassium carbonate. A_r K = 39, A_r C = 12, A_r O = 16

b. Calculate the number of moles of potassium carbonate in the reaction.

c. Using the large numbers in the chemical equation, how many moles of potassium chloride could be produced?

d. Calculate the relative formula mass of potassium chloride A_r K = 39, A_r Cl = 35.5

e. Calculate the mass of potassium chloride that could be produced if the percentage yield is 100%.

f. The percentage yield was 60%. Calculate the mass of potassium chloride produced.

Atom Economy

1. The two reactions below both produce calcium oxide.

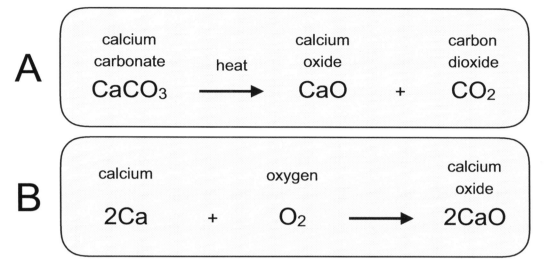

In both cases, the desired product is calcium oxide.

Explain in terms of atoms why reaction A is less efficient than reaction B.

2. The efficiency of a chemical reaction is determined by calculating the atom economy (which is also called the atom utilisation).

a. Write the definition for atom economy in the space below.

b. State one economic advantage and one environmental advantage of calculating the atom economy for a reaction.

• Economic advantage:

• Environmental advantage:

$$\text{Atom economy} = \frac{\text{relative formula mass of desired products (from equation)}}{\text{relative formula mass of all reactants (from equation)}} \times 100$$

Exam tip: The words "from equation" mean that big numbers count when calculating atom economy.

3. Explain why the atom economy of reaction B on the previous page must be 100%.

4. Calculate the atom economy of the reactions below (* shows the desired product).

a.   LiOH   +   HCl $\longrightarrow$ *LiCl   + H_2O

(A_r Li = 7, A_r O = 16, A_r H = 1, A_r Cl = 35.5)

b.   ZnO   +   2Li $\longrightarrow$ Li_2O +   *Zn

(A_r Zn = 65, A_r O = 16, A_r Li = 7)

c. Fe_2O_3 +   3CO $\longrightarrow$ *2Fe   + $3CO_2$

(A_r Fe = 56, A_r O = 16, A_r C = 12)

5. Explain why we cannot have an atom economy greater than 100%.

Using Concentration of Solutions 1

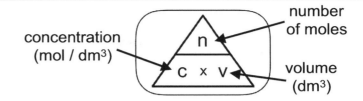

concentration
(mol / dm³)

number
of moles

volume
(dm³)

1. Calculate the number of moles in the following solutions.

a. 0.5 dm³ of sodium hydroxide solution with a concentration of 2 mol / dm³.

b. 200 cm³ of calcium chloride solution with a concentration of 4 mol / dm³.

2. A solution of lithium bromide (M_r = 87) has a concentration of 1.0 mol / dm³.

a. Calculate the number of moles of lithium bromide in 0.5 dm³ of the solution.

b. Calculate the mass of lithium bromide in 0.5 dm³ of the solution.

3. A solution of sodium carbonate (M_r = 106) has a concentration of 2.5 mol / dm³.

a. Calculate the number of moles of sodium carbonate in 3 dm³ of the solution.

b. Calculate the mass of sodium carbonate in 3 dm³ of the solution.

Using Concentration of Solutions 2

1. 0.05 dm³ of calcium hydroxide solution (concentration 0.1 mol / dm³) reacted with 0.075 dm³ of copper (II) chloride solution.

The equation is shown below.

calcium hydroxide		copper (II) chloride		copper (II) hydroxide		calcium chloride
$Ca(OH)_2$ $_{(aq)}$	+	$CuCl_2$ $_{(aq)}$	⟶	$Cu(OH)_2$ $_{(s)}$	+	$CaCl_2$ $_{(aq)}$

a. Calculate the number of moles of calcium hydroxide in the reaction.

b. Using the large numbers in the chemical equation, state how many moles of copper (II) chloride react with this?

c. Calculate the concentration of the copper (II) chloride solution (to 3 significant figures).

2. 0.02 dm³ of silver nitrate solution (concentration 0.15 mol / dm³) reacted with 15 cm³ of sodium iodide solution.

The equation is shown below.

silver nitrate		sodium iodide		sodium nitrate		silver iodide
$AgNO_3$ $_{(aq)}$	+	NaI $_{(aq)}$	⟶	$NaNO_3$ $_{(aq)}$	+	AgI $_{(s)}$

a. Calculate the number of moles of silver nitrate in the reaction.

b. Using the large numbers in the chemical equation, state how many moles of sodium iodide react with this?

c. Calculate the concentration of the sodium iodide solution.

3. 0.04 dm³ of sodium carbonate solution (concentration 0.2 mol / dm³) reacted with 0.01 dm³ of hydrochloric acid.

The equation is shown below.

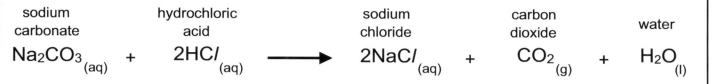

| sodium carbonate | | hydrochloric acid | | sodium chloride | | carbon dioxide | | water |

$$Na_2CO_3 \text{ (aq)} \quad + \quad 2HCl \text{ (aq)} \quad \longrightarrow \quad 2NaCl \text{ (aq)} \quad + \quad CO_2 \text{ (g)} \quad + \quad H_2O \text{ (l)}$$

a. Calculate the number of moles of sodium carbonate in the reaction.

b. Using the large numbers in the chemical equation, state how many moles of hydrochloric acid react with this?

c. Calculate the concentration of the hydrochloric acid.

---

4. 0.015 dm³ of potassium bromide solution (concentration 0.3 mol / dm³) reacted with 0.02 dm³ of lead nitrate solution.

The equation is shown below.

| lead nitrate | | potassium bromide | | lead bromide | | potassium nitrate |

$$Pb(NO_3)_2 \text{ (aq)} \quad + \quad 2KBr \text{ (aq)} \quad \longrightarrow \quad PbBr_2 \text{ (s)} \quad + \quad 2KNO_3 \text{ (aq)}$$

a. Calculate the number of moles of potassium bromide in the reaction.

b. Using the large numbers in the chemical equation, state how many moles of lead nitrate react with this.

c. Calculate the concentration of the lead nitrate solution (to 3 significant figures).

Using Gas Volumes 1

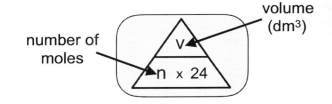

1. What do scientists mean by room temperature and pressure (RTP)?

2. Calculate the volumes in dm³ of the following gases at RTP.

a. 2 moles of carbon dioxide.

b. 0.5 moles of nitrogen.

c. 10 moles of ammonia.

3. Calculate the volumes in dm³ of the following gases (at RTP).

For each of these questions, you will need to calculate the number of moles first.

a. 120 g of neon. A_r Ne = 20.

b. 92 g of nitrogen dioxide NO_2. M_r NO_2 = 46.

Using Gas Volumes 2

1. 48g of magnesium was reacted with sulfuric acid.

The reaction is shown below.

magnesium		sulfuric acid		magnesium sulfate		hydrogen
$Mg_{(s)}$	+	$H_2SO_{4\,(aq)}$ $\longrightarrow$		$MgSO_{4\,(aq)}$	+	$H_{2\,(g)}$

a. Calculate the number of moles of magnesium used in the reaction. A_r Mg = 24.

b. Using the large numbers in the chemical equation, state how many moles of hydrogen gas will be produced.

c. Calculate the volume of the hydrogen gas produced (assume that the reaction takes place at room temperature and pressure).

2. Hydrogen peroxide breaks down to produce oxygen gas.

hydrogen peroxide	catalyst	water		oxygen
$2H_2O_{2\,(l)}$	$\longrightarrow$	$2H_2O_{(l)}$	+	$O_{2\,(g)}$

a. In this reaction, 204 g of hydrogen peroxide was used.

Calculate the number of moles of hydrogen peroxide used in the reaction. Mr H_2O_2 = 34.

b. Using the large numbers in the chemical equation, state how many moles of oxygen gas will be produced.

c. Calculate the volume of the oxygen gas produced (assume room temperature and pressure).

3. Carbon dioxide gas reacts with sodium hydroxide.

The reaction is shown below.

carbon dioxide		sodium hydroxide		sodium hydrogen carbonate
$CO_{2\ (g)}$	+	$NaOH_{\ (s)}$	$\longrightarrow$	$NaHCO_{3\ (s)}$

a. In this reaction, 160 g of sodium hydroxide was used.

Calculate the number of moles of sodium hydroxide in the reaction. M_r NaOH = 40.

b. Using the large numbers in the chemical equation, state how many moles of carbon dioxide gas took part in the reaction.

c. Calculate the volume of carbon dioxide gas that took part (assume room temperature and pressure).

---

4. Oxygen gas reacts with potassium.

The reaction is shown below.

oxygen		potassium		potassium oxide
$O_{2\ (g)}$	+	$4K_{\ (s)}$	$\longrightarrow$	$2K_2O_{\ (s)}$

a. In this reaction, 376 g of potassium oxide was made.

Calculate the number of moles of potassium oxide made. M_r K$_2$O = 94.

b. Using the large numbers in the chemical equation, state how many moles of oxygen gas took part in the reaction.

c. Calculate the volume of oxygen gas that took part (assume room temperature and pressure).

Chapter 4: Chemical Changes

- Describe how metals react with oxygen.

- Use the results of experiments to construct a simple reactivity series.

- Describe how metals can be extracted from their compounds by displacement by a more reactive element.

- State whether a reaction is oxidation or reduction in terms of oxygen.

- Identify from a chemical reaction whether oxidation or reduction has taken place in terms of the transfer of electrons.

- Describe what is meant by an acid and an alkali.

- State pH values for an acidic, alkaline or neutral solution.

- State the equation for the neutralisation reaction between an acid and an alkali.

- Describe what is produced when an acid reacts with a metal.

- Describe what is produced when an acid reacts with a base, an alkali or a metal carbonate.

- Describe how to make a pure, dry sample of a soluble salt from an insoluble metal oxide or metal carbonate (required practical).

- Describe what is meant by a strong / weak and concentrated / dilute acid and how these affect the pH of a solution.

- Describe how to carry out a titration to determine the reacting volumes of a strong acid or a strong alkali in a neutralisation reaction (required practical).

- Use titration results to determine the concentration of an acid or alkali.

- Describe what is taking place at the cathode and anode during electrolysis and write half equations for reactions from given information.

- Describe how aluminium can be produced by the electrolysis of molten aluminium oxide.

- Predict the products at the cathode and anode from the electrolysis of aqueous solutions.

- Describe how to identify the products of the electrolysis of aqueous sodium chloride and aqueous copper chloride (required practical).

Reactions of Metals with Oxygen

1. Complete the following reactions to show how metals react with oxygen.

lithium   +   oxygen   ⟶   _____

_____   +   oxygen   ⟶   calcium oxide

sodium   +   _____   ⟶   sodium oxide

2. Explain how the three reactions above are all examples of oxidation.

3. The equation below shows the reaction between zinc oxide and potassium.

zinc oxide   +   potassium   ⟶   potassium oxide   +   zinc

In this reaction, which element is being reduced?

Explain your answer.

4. Identify what is being oxidised and being reduced in the following equations.

aluminium   +   lead oxide   ⟶   aluminium oxide   +   lead

oxidised = _____   reduced = _____

tin oxide   +   magnesium   ⟶   magnesium oxide   +   tin

oxidised = _____   reduced = _____

zinc   +   iron oxide   ⟶   iron   +   zinc oxide

oxidised = _____   reduced = _____

The Reactivity Series

1. In chapter one, we saw that Group 1 metals react very rapidly with water at room temperature.

a. Complete the equations below to show how lithium, sodium and potassium react.

lithium + water ⟶ [   ] + [   ]

sodium + water ⟶ [   ] + [   ]

potassium + water ⟶ [   ] + [   ]

b. Compare the reactivity of these three metals.

---

2. The reactions of other metals are shown below.

Use these reactions and question 1 to complete the reactivity series on the right.

Iron does not react with room temperature water. Iron reacts slowly with dilute acid.

Magnesium does not react with room temperature water but it reacts rapidly with dilute acid.

Copper does not react with room temperature water or with dilute acid.

Zinc does not react with room temperature water. Zinc reacts quite rapidly with dilute acid.

Calcium reacts quite rapidly with water at room temperature.

Reactivity Series

[   ]

[   ]

[   ]

[   ]

[   ]

Carbon

[   ]

[   ]

Hydrogen

[   ]

Remember that when metals react, the metal atom loses electrons and forms a positive ion. The reactivity tells us how easily the atoms lose electrons and form positive ions.

Extraction of Metals

1. Some metals can be found as nuggets in the Earth's crust.

A good example is gold.

a. What does this tell us about the reactivity of these metals?

b. Is it easy or difficult for these elements to lose electrons?

Explain your answer.

2. Most metals are found in the Earth's crust already reacted with other elements such as oxygen.

To extract the metal, we displace it. Complete the following sentence.

> A _____ reactive element will push out (displace)
> a _____ reactive element from its compound.

3. Iron is extracted from iron oxide using carbon.

The equation for this reaction is shown below.

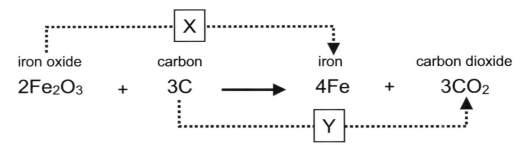

Reactivity Series
Potassium
Sodium
Lithium
Calcium
Magnesium
Carbon
Zinc
Iron
Hydrogen
Copper

iron oxide   carbon   iron   carbon dioxide

$$2Fe_2O_3 \quad + \quad 3C \quad \longrightarrow \quad 4Fe \quad + \quad 3CO_2$$

a. Use the reactivity series to explain why carbon can displace iron.

b. Explain why hydrogen could not be used to extract iron.

c. State which process (X or Y) shows oxidation and which shows reduction.

Explain your answer in each case.

4. All of the following equations show potential displacement reactions.

- Use the reactivity series to determine if each reaction is possible.

- For each of the possible reactions, state what is undergoing oxidation and what is undergoing reduction.

a.   zinc oxide   sodium   zinc   sodium oxide

$$ZnO \quad + \quad 2Na \quad \longrightarrow \quad Zn \quad + \quad Na_2O$$

b.   magnesium oxide   iron   magnesium   iron oxide

$$3MgO \quad + \quad 2Fe \quad \longrightarrow \quad 3Mg \quad + \quad Fe_2O_3$$

c.   copper oxide   lithium   copper   lithium oxide

$$CuO \quad + \quad 2Li \quad \longrightarrow \quad Cu \quad + \quad Li_2O$$

Oxidation and Reduction in terms of Electrons

1. Complete the following to show what is meant by oxidation and reduction in terms of electrons.

O .... **I** ...... **L** .... (of electrons)

R .... **I** ...... **G** .... (of electrons)

2. State whether each of the following half equations show oxidation or reduction.

Explain your answer in each case.

$$F \quad + \quad 1\,e^- \quad \longrightarrow \quad F^-$$

$$Al \quad \longrightarrow \quad Al^{3+} \quad + \quad 3\,e^-$$

3. Complete the following half equations to show the number of electrons transferred in each reaction.

In each case, state whether the reaction shows oxidation or reduction.

$$Se \quad + \quad \underline{\quad}\,e^- \quad \longrightarrow \quad Se^{2-} \qquad \text{oxidation / reduction}$$

$$Mn \quad \longrightarrow \quad Mn^{4+} \quad + \quad \underline{\quad}\,e^- \qquad \text{oxidation / reduction}$$

$$Br \quad + \quad \underline{\quad}\,e^- \quad \longrightarrow \quad Br^- \qquad \text{oxidation / reduction}$$

$$Cr \quad \longrightarrow \quad Cr^{2+} \quad + \quad \underline{\quad}\,e^- \qquad \text{oxidation / reduction}$$

4. Each of the following displacement reactions show oxidation and reduction.

- State what is being oxidised and what is being reduced. The relevant ions are shown to help you.
- The first example has been done for you.
- Write half equations to show oxidation and reduction for each question.

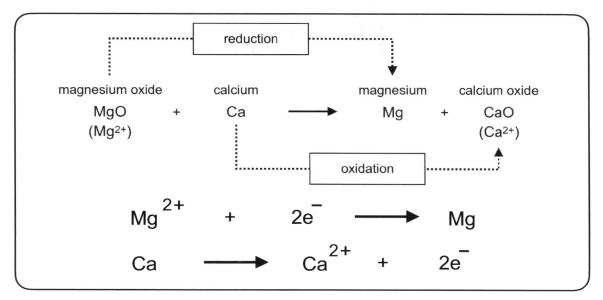

a.

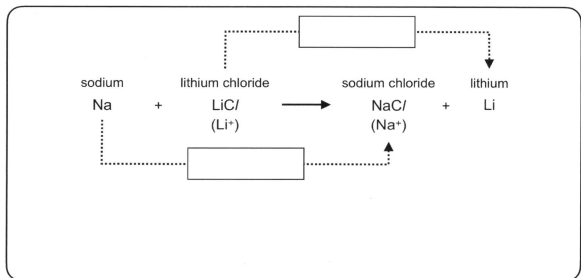

b.

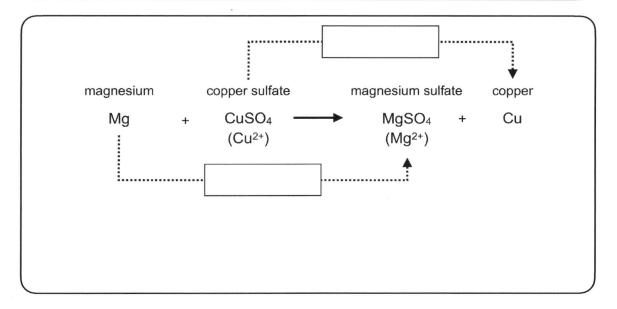

Acids and Alkalis

1. The boxes show the formulas of three acids.

a. Which element do all of these acids have in common?

b. What do the letters (aq) tell us about these acids?

hydrochloric acid
HCl (aq)

sulfuric acid
H_2SO_4 (aq)

nitric acid
HNO_3 (aq)

---

2. In aqueous solution, all three acids split (ionise).

a. Complete the reactions to show what is produced when acid molecules split.

$HCl_{(aq)}$ → _____ (aq) + $Cl^-_{(aq)}$

$H_2SO_{4\,(aq)}$ → _____ (aq) + $SO_4^{2-}_{(aq)}$

$HNO_{3\,(aq)}$ → _____ (aq) + $NO_3^-_{(aq)}$

b. What is produced when every acid molecule splits?

---

3. Bases are molecules which can neutralise acids.

Bases which dissolve in water are called alkalis.

a. What is produced when alkalis split in aqueous solution?

b. The neutralisation reaction between any acid and any alkali is shown on the right.

Fill in the spaces to complete the reaction.

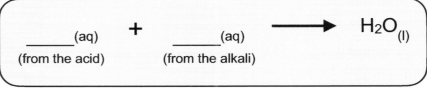

_____(aq) + _____(aq) → $H_2O_{(l)}$
(from the acid)   (from the alkali)

c. Write the pH values of the following:

Acids	Neutral	Alkalis

d. What could a scientist use to determine the pH of a solution?

Acids Reacting with Metals

1. The reaction between magnesium and hydrochloric acid is shown below.

							Reactivity Series

magnesium   hydrochloric acid   _____   hydrogen

Mg   +   2HC*l* $\longrightarrow$ MgC*l*$_2$ +   H$_2$

Reactivity Series

Potassium

Sodium

Lithium

Calcium

Magnesium

Carbon

Zinc

Iron

Hydrogen

Copper

a. Write the name of the salt produced in this reaction.

b. Use the reactivity series and the above equation to show how this is an example of a displacement reaction.

Exam tip: You are only required to know the reactions of magnesium, zinc and iron with hydrochloric acid and sulfuric acid.

2. Write the products of the following reactions between metals and acids.

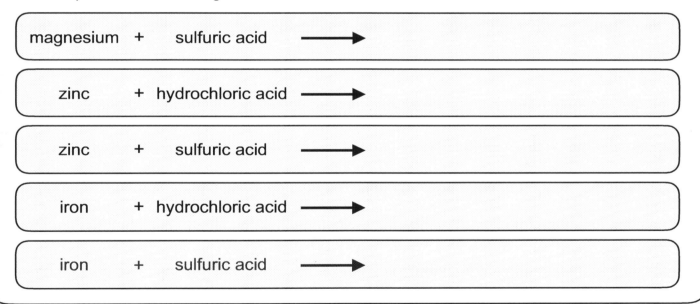

magnesium   +   sulfuric acid $\longrightarrow$

zinc   +   hydrochloric acid $\longrightarrow$

zinc   +   sulfuric acid $\longrightarrow$

iron   +   hydrochloric acid $\longrightarrow$

iron   +   sulfuric acid $\longrightarrow$

3. Magnesium reacts rapidly with dilute acids, zinc reacts quite rapidly and iron reacts slowly.

a. Use the reactivity series to explain this.

b. Explain why copper does not react with dilute acids.

Acids Reacting with Metals 2

1. Acids split (ionise) in aqueous solution. This is shown for hydrochloric acid and sulfuric acid.

a. Complete the equations to show the first product in each case.

$$HCl_{(aq)} \longrightarrow \underline{\hspace{2cm}}_{(aq)} + Cl^{-}_{(aq)}$$

$$H_2SO_{4\,(aq)} \longrightarrow \underline{\hspace{2cm}}_{(aq)} + SO_4^{2-}_{(aq)}$$

b. Complete the sentence below.

In aqueous solution, all acids split to release the _____ ion H^+

2. When acids react with metals, a salt and hydrogen gas are produced.

This is shown below for the reaction between magnesium and sulfuric acid.

magnesium	sulfuric acid		magnesium sulfate	hydrogen

$$Mg_{(s)} + H_2SO_{4\,(aq)} \longrightarrow MgSO_{4\,(aq)} + H_{2\,(g)}$$

a. Complete the half equation below to show what happens when the magnesium atom reacts.

$$Mg_{(s)} \longrightarrow Mg^{2+}_{(aq)} + \underline{\hspace{2cm}}$$

b. Explain how this shows that the magnesium has been oxidised.

c. The diagram shows the electron energy levels for magnesium.

Use this to explain why magnesium atoms undergo oxidation.

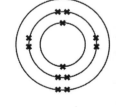

magnesium

d. The half equation below shows how the hydrogen ions from the acid react.

Explain how this shows that the hydrogen ions have been reduced.

$$2H^+_{(aq)} + 2e^- \longrightarrow H_{2\,(g)}$$

Three Reactions of Acids

1. The chemicals below are all bases.

However, sodium hydroxide is also an alkali.

Copper oxide	Iron (III) oxide	Sodium hydroxide

a. Complete the definition of a base below.

> Bases can _____ acids, producing a _____ and water

b. Explain how copper oxide and iron (III) oxide are bases but sodium hydroxide is both a base and an alkali.

2. The equations below show a base and an alkali reacting with acids.

a. Complete the equations to show the products in both cases.

copper oxide   hydrochloric acid   _____ _____

$CuO_{(s)}$ + $2\ HCl_{(aq)}$ ⟶ $CuCl_{2\ (aq)}$ + $H_2O_{(l)}$

sodium hydroxide   nitric acid   _____ _____

$NaOH_{(aq)}$ + $HNO_{3\ (aq)}$ ⟶ $NaNO_{3\ (aq)}$ + $H_2O_{(l)}$

b. Name the two products formed when any base or alkali react with an acid.

3. The equation below shows a metal carbonate reacting with an acid.

a. Complete the equation to show the three products of this reaction.

potassium carbonate   sulfuric acid   _____ _____ _____

$K_2CO_{3\ (s)}$ + $H_2SO_{4(aq)}$ ⟶ $K_2SO_{4(aq)}$ + $CO_{2(g)}$ + $H_2O_{(l)}$

b. Name the three products formed when any metal carbonate reacts with an acid.

Required Practical: Making Soluble Salts

1. In this practical we are making copper sulfate. The formula is shown below.

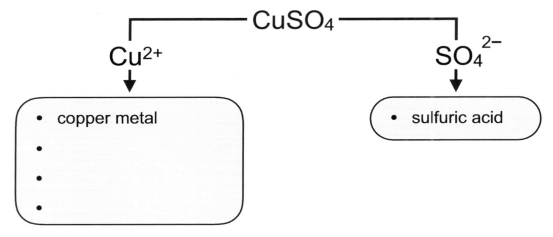

a. Copper sulfate contains the positive copper ion Cu^{2+}.

Fill in the boxes to show four possible reactants which provide this (the first has been completed for you).

b. Explain why we cannot use copper metal to produce copper sulfate using dilute sulfuric acid.

c. Which acids would we need to use to produce the following salts?

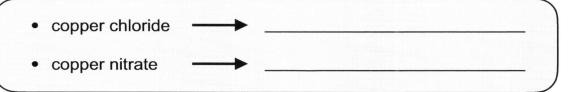

2. In this reaction, we use a fixed volume of sulfuric acid.

a. By using a fixed volume of acid, we make the acid the limiting reactant.

What is meant by the limiting reactant?

b. Why is it important that there is no acid left at the end of the reaction?

c. What would be the pH of the product if there was unreacted acid left over?

| pH 0-6 | pH 7 | pH 8-14 |

3. This practical has several important stages.

You need to learn them as this could be a 6 mark exam question.

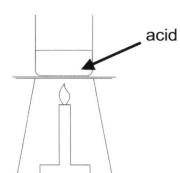

acid

First we need to heat our acid until it is almost boiling.

The reaction is faster when the acid is hot.

a. Why is it important that the acid is not boiling?

We now add copper oxide powder and stir with a glass rod.

b. Why does the solution turn blue?

copper oxide

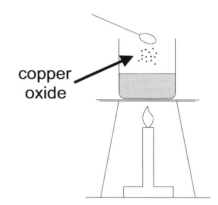

We continue adding copper oxide until the reaction stops.

c. How do we know when the reaction has stopped?

d. Why does the reaction stop at this stage?

We now filter away any unreacted copper oxide using a filter funnel and filter paper.

e. Label the diagram to show.

- The unreacted copper oxide.
- The filtrate (copper sulfate solution).

We now need to evaporate the water from the copper sulfate solution to allow crystals to form.

f. What name do scientists give to this process?

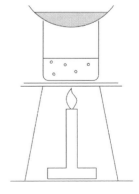

g. Once the crystals have formed, we need to dry them.

Describe how we carry this out.

Strong and Weak Acids

1. The equations below show hydrochloric acid and carbonic acid in aqueous solution.

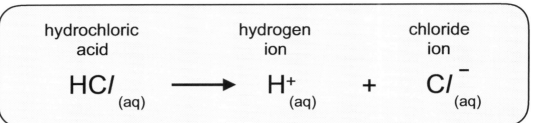

hydrochloric acid		hydrogen ion		chloride ion
$HCl_{(aq)}$	$\longrightarrow$	$H^+_{(aq)}$	$+$	$Cl^-_{(aq)}$

carbonic acid		hydrogen ion		hydrogen carbonate ion
$H_2CO_{3(aq)}$	$\rightleftharpoons$	$H^+_{(aq)}$	$+$	$HCO_3^-{}_{(aq)}$

Use these equations to explain why:

- Hydrochloric acid is an example of a strong acid.

- Carbonic acid is an example of a weak acid.

2. You need to be able to state examples of strong and weak acids. Six different acids are shown below.

Next to each one, write S for "strong" or W for "weak".

ethanoic acid	hydrochloric acid	citric acid

nitric acid	carbonic acid	sulfuric acid

3. Scientists often use the pH scale when talking about an acid.

a. What information does the pH scale give us about acids?

b. Complete the paragraph using the words below.

magnitude   **lower**   **concentration**   **increases**

As the pH scale decreases by one unit, the _____ of hydrogen ions (H^+)

_____ by 10 times. Scientists call a 10x change one order of_____.

Strong acids have a_____ pH than weak acids for a given concentration.

c. Explain why strong acids have a lower pH than weak acids.

---

4. State the order of magnitude difference in the H^+ concentration between the following pH values (the first has been done for you).

| 6 → 8 | pH 6 has a 100x greater H^+ concentration than pH 8 (ie two orders of magnitude greater) |

| 1 → 2 | |

| 2 → 6 | |

---

5. What do you think will happen to the pH of an acid if we add more water?

Circle the correct answer and then explain this in the space below.

(The pH would not change)   (The pH would increase)   (The pH would decrease)

Explanation:

Required Practical: Titration

This practical has several important stages.

1. First we use a pipette to transfer the alkali (with a known concentration) into a conical flask.

a. Why is a conical flask better to use than a beaker?

b. Explain why a pipette is used to measure the volume of alkali.

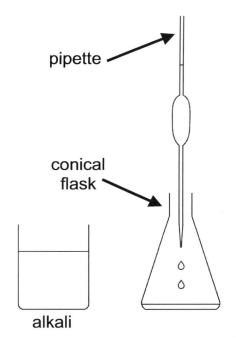

pipette

conical flask

alkali

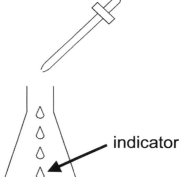

indicator

2. We now add five drops of an indicator such as methyl orange.

Suggest why methyl orange is used rather than universal indicator.

3. Next we place the conical flask on a white tile.

Explain why using a white tile gives us more valid results.

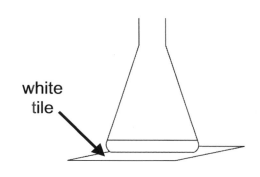

white tile

4. Now we fill a burette with our acid (unknown concentration) and gradually add the acid to the alkali.

a. Explain why a burette is used to measure the volume of acid.

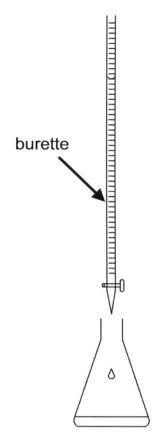

burette

b. Using methyl orange indicator, what colour change will we see when neutralisation takes place?

c. What should we do when we start to see a colour change?

Explain why this is important.

d. Why is it important that we swirl the solution while adding the acid to the alkali?

---

5. Finally we read the volume of acid that we added to our alkali for neutralisation to take place.

It is important that we take our reading at the bottom of the meniscus.

a. Using the diagram, explain what is meant by the meniscus.

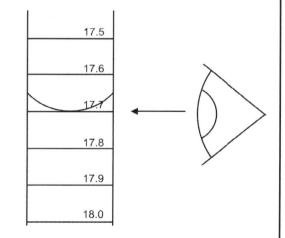

17.5

17.6

17.7

17.8

17.9

18.0

b. Read the volume of acid shown in the diagram.

c. We normally repeat our titration until we get two readings within 0.1 cm³ (these are called concordant readings).

What do scientists then do with concordant readings?

Titration Calculations 1

Exam tip: Remember to convert cm³ to dm³ by dividing by 1000.

concentration (mol / dm³)

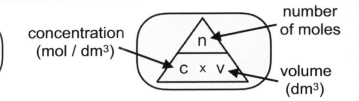

number of moles

volume (dm³)

1. The equation below shows the reaction between hydrochloric acid and the alkali lithium hydroxide.

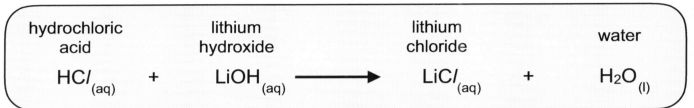

| hydrochloric acid | | lithium hydroxide | | lithium chloride | | water |
| $HCl_{(aq)}$ | + | $LiOH_{(aq)}$ | ⟶ | $LiCl_{(aq)}$ | + | $H_2O_{(l)}$ |

15 cm³ of 0.5 mol / dm³ hydrochloric acid was required to neutralise 25 cm³ of lithium hydroxide.

a. What name do scientists give to this kind of reaction?

displacement   oxidation   neutralisation

b. Calculate the volume of the hydrochloric acid in dm³.

c. Calculate the total number of moles of hydrochloric acid in the reaction.

d. Using the large numbers in the chemical equation, determine the number of moles of lithium hydroxide that reacted.

e. Calculate the concentration of the lithium hydroxide in mol / dm³.

f. Calculate the concentration of the lithium hydroxide in g / dm³. M_r LiOH = 24

2. The equation below shows the reaction between nitric acid and the alkali potassium hydroxide.

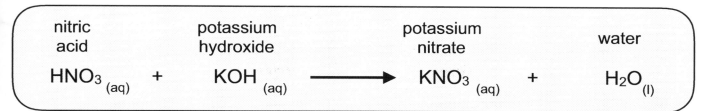

nitric acid		potassium hydroxide		potassium nitrate		water
$HNO_3{}_{(aq)}$	+	$KOH{}_{(aq)}$	$\longrightarrow$	$KNO_3{}_{(aq)}$	+	$H_2O{}_{(l)}$

25 cm³ of 0.8 mol / dm³ potassium hydroxide was neutralised by 18.5 cm³ of nitric acid.

a. Calculate the volume of the potassium hydroxide in dm³.

b. Calculate the total number of moles of potassium hydroxide in the reaction.

c. Using the large numbers in the chemical equation, determine the number of moles of nitric acid that reacted.

d. Calculate the concentration of the nitric acid in mol / dm³.

State your answer to 3 significant figures.

e. Calculate the relative formula mass of nitric acid. A_r H = 1. A_r N = 14. A_r O = 16.

f. Using your answers to parts d and e, calculate the concentration of the nitric acid in g / dm³.

State your answer to 3 significant figures.

We've now seen examples where the balancing numbers are the same for both the acid and alkali. In the next section, we'll look at examples where the balancing numbers are not the same and how we deal with this.

Titration Calculations 2

1. The equation below shows the reaction between hydrochloric acid and the alkali barium hydroxide.

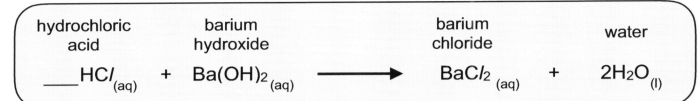

hydrochloric acid		barium hydroxide			barium chloride		water
____ $HCl_{(aq)}$	+	$Ba(OH)_{2(aq)}$	$\longrightarrow$		$BaCl_{2(aq)}$	+	$2H_2O_{(l)}$

18 cm³ of 1 mol / dm³ hydrochloric acid was neutralised by 12 cm³ of barium hydroxide.

a. Balance the equation by inserting a large number in the space provided.

b. Calculate the volume of hydrochloric acid in dm³.

c. Calculate the total number of moles of hydrochloric acid in the reaction.

d. Using the large numbers in the chemical equation, determine the number of moles of barium hydroxide that reacted.

e. Calculate the concentration of the barium hydroxide in mol / dm³.

f. Calculate the relative formula mass of barium hydroxide. A_r Ba = 137, A_r O = 16, A_r H = 1.

g. Using your answers to parts e and f, calculate the concentration of the barium hydroxide in g / dm³.

2. The equation below shows the reaction between sulfuric acid and the alkali sodium hydroxide.

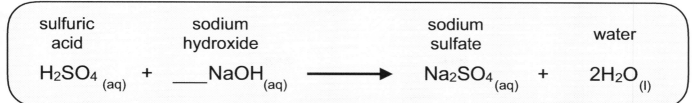

| sulfuric acid | | sodium hydroxide | | | sodium sulfate | | water |

$$H_2SO_4 _{(aq)} \quad + \quad \underline{}NaOH _{(aq)} \longrightarrow Na_2SO_4 _{(aq)} \quad + \quad 2H_2O _{(l)}$$

14 cm³ of 2 mol / dm³ sulfuric acid was neutralised by 16 cm³ of sodium hydroxide.

a. Balance the equation by inserting a large number in the space provided.

b. Calculate the volume of sulfuric acid in dm³.

c. Calculate the total number of moles of sulfuric acid in the reaction.

d. Using the large numbers in the chemical equation, determine the number of moles of sodium hydroxide that reacted.

e. Calculate the concentration of the sodium hydroxide in mol / dm³.

f. Calculate the relative formula mass of sodium hydroxide. A_r Na = 23. A_r O = 16. A_r H = 1.

g. Using your answers to parts e and f, calculate the concentration of the sodium hydroxide in g / dm³.

Introducing Electrolysis

1. When lead reacts with bromine, it forms the ionic compound lead bromide (PbBr₂).

Lead bromide contains the lead ion (Pb²⁺) and the bromide ion (Br⁻).

a. The diagram shows the structure of solid lead bromide.

Complete the diagram by labelling the electrostatic forces of attraction.

b. Ionic compounds cannot conduct electricity when they are in their solid state but can conduct electricity when melted or dissolved in water.

Explain why.

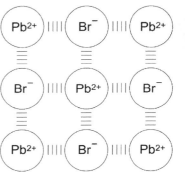

Exam tip: Remember that it is the ions that move when an ionic compound conducts electricity. Many students incorrectly refer to electrons moving and lose the mark in the exam.

c. What do scientists call a liquid or solution that can conduct electricity?

electrodes

electrolyte

electrolysate

2. During electrolysis, the electric current passes into the electrolyte through electrodes. These are made from graphite or from metal.

a. Explain why graphite or a metal are used as electrodes.

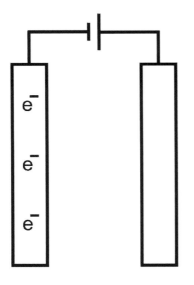

b. On the diagram, label the cathode and the anode.

c. In terms of electrons, why is the cathode negative and the anode positive?

3. Remember that ionic compounds contain a positive metal ion and a negative non-metal ion.

You need to consider both of these ions during electrolysis.

The diagram shows the ions in lead bromide at the cathode and the anode.

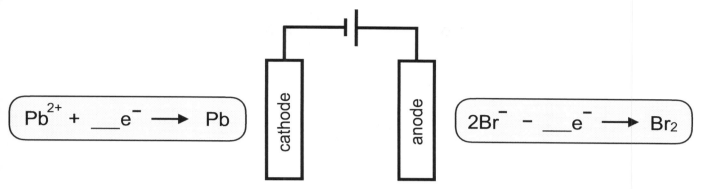

$$Pb^{2+} + \underline{\quad}e^- \longrightarrow Pb$$

$$2Br^- - \underline{\quad}e^- \longrightarrow Br_2$$

a. During electrolysis, the Pb^{2+} ions are attracted to the cathode and the Br^- ions are attracted to the anode.

Explain why.

b. Complete the diagram to show the number of electrons transferred at each electrode.

c. Fill in the boxes below to show whether each reaction is an example of oxidation or reduction.

In each case, explain your answer.

Reaction at the cathode

(reduction)   (oxidation)

Reaction at the anode

(reduction)   (oxidation)

d. The reaction at the anode can be written like this instead:

$$2Br^- \longrightarrow Br_2 + 2e^-$$

Explain how this shows the same reaction as the one shown above.

Electrolysis of Aluminium Oxide

1. The reactivity series is shown on the left.

Reactivity Series

Potassium*
Sodium*
Lithium*
Calcium*
Magnesium*
Aluminium*
Carbon
Zinc
Iron
Copper

a. Explain why carbon cannot be used to extract metals shown with ✱ .

Exam tip: Remember that electrolysis is used to extract every metal above carbon in the reactivity series.

b. Why is aluminium a useful metal for making aircraft bodies?

c. Before aluminium oxide is melted, the chemical cryolite is added.

Complete the paragraph below to explain why cryolite is used.

energy   melting   money   lowers   electrostatic

Aluminium oxide has an extremely high _____ point (around 2000°C).

This is due to the very strong _____ forces of attraction between the ions.

Cryolite_____ the melting point. This reduces the amount of_____

needed for melting and saves_____ .

2. During the electrolysis of aluminium oxide, graphite is used as the electrodes.

a. Describe two properties of graphite which make it useful as electrodes.

b. Explain why molten aluminium oxide is a good conductor of electricity.

3. The diagram below shows the electrodes during the electrolysis of aluminium oxide.

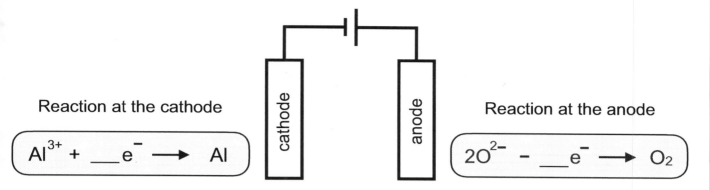

Reaction at the cathode

$$Al^{3+} + \underline{}e^{-} \longrightarrow Al$$

cathode

anode

Reaction at the anode

$$2O^{2-} - \underline{}e^{-} \longrightarrow O_2$$

a. The aluminium ions are attracted to the cathode and the oxide ions are attracted to the anode.

Explain why.

b. Complete the half equations above to show how electrons are transferred.

c. Which of the above half equations shows an oxidation reaction?

Explain your answer.

Exam tip: The half equation for the anode can also be written as:

$$2O^{2-} \longrightarrow O_2 + 4e^{-}$$

Remember that this shows the same process as the half equation above. The oxygen ions are losing electrons to form oxygen molecules (O_2).

d. Oxygen is produced at the anode.

Explain why the anode must be replaced regularly.

e. Describe two reasons why it is expensive to extract metals using electrolysis of molten compounds.

Electrolysis of Aqueous Solutions 1

1. Aqueous solutions are dissolved in water.

Water molecules naturally ionise (split).

Complete the equation below to show how water molecules ionise.

$$H_2O \rightleftharpoons \underset{\substack{\text{hydrogen} \\ \text{ion}}}{\hspace{3cm}} + \underset{\substack{\text{hydroxide} \\ \text{ion}}}{\hspace{3cm}}$$

2. A good example of an aqueous solution is copper sulfate solution.

The ions in copper sulfate solution are shown below.

$$Cu^{2+} \qquad H^{+} \qquad SO_4^{2-} \qquad OH^{-}$$

a. Circle the ions that will be attracted to the cathode and explain your answer below.

b. Use the reactivity series to explain why copper (and not hydrogen) is produced at the cathode.

c. Complete the half equation to show the reduction of copper at the cathode.

$$Cu^{2+} \quad + \quad \underline{\hspace{2cm}} \quad \longrightarrow \quad Cu$$

d. Complete the half equations to show why oxygen is produced at the anode.

$$4OH^{-} \longrightarrow \underline{\hspace{1.5cm}} + 2H_2O + 4e^{-}$$

$$4OH^{-} - 4e^{-} \longrightarrow \underline{\hspace{1.5cm}} + 2H_2O$$

Exam tip: Remember that these two half equations show the same process.

e. Why is platinum often used as the electrode during electrolysis?

Reactivity Series
Potassium
Sodium
Calcium
Magnesium
Zinc
Iron
Lead
Hydrogen
Copper
Mercury
Silver

Electrolysis of Aqueous Solutions 2

1. Sodium chloride solution contains four main ions.

These are shown below.

$$Na^+ \qquad H^+ \qquad Cl^- \qquad OH^-$$

a. Write "C" next to the ions that will be attracted to the cathode and "A" next to the ions that will be attracted to the anode.

b. Use the reactivity series to explain why hydrogen is produced at the cathode and not sodium.

c. Complete the half equation to show the reduction of hydrogen at the cathode.

$$2H^+ \quad + \quad \underline{\qquad} \quad \longrightarrow \quad H_2$$

Reactivity Series
Potassium
Sodium
Calcium
Magnesium
Zinc
Iron
Lead
Hydrogen
Copper
Mercury
Silver

d. Explain why we show this reaction for two hydrogen ions rather than one.

e. In the electrolysis of sodium chloride solution, why is chlorine gas produced at the anode rather than oxygen?

f. Complete the half equations to show the oxidation of chloride ions at the anode.

$$2Cl^- \quad \longrightarrow \quad Cl_2 \quad + \quad \underline{\qquad}$$

$$2Cl^- \quad - \quad \underline{\qquad} \quad \longrightarrow \quad Cl_2$$

Exam tip: Remember that these two half equations show the same process.

Exam tip: Learn these rules for the electrolysis of aqueous solutions:

1. The metal is produced at the cathode if the metal ion is less reactive than hydrogen. Otherwise hydrogen is produced at the cathode.
2. If the compound contains a halide ion, then the halogen is produced at the anode. Otherwise oxygen is produced at the anode.

Required Practical: Electrolysis

1. In this practical, we are electrolysing two different solutions and looking at the products.

First we pour around 50cm³ of copper (II) chloride solution into a beaker
and connect this to a power pack using graphite electrodes.

a. Graphite electrodes are inert. What does this mean?

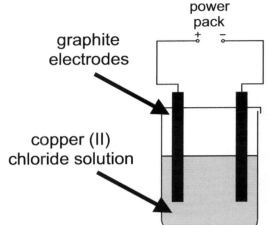

graphite
electrodes

power
pack

copper (II)
chloride solution

b. Use the reactivity series on the previous page to state which
element is produced at the cathode.

Explain your answer.

c. Explain why chlorine gas and not oxygen gas is produced at the anode.

d. How do we test for chlorine gas? Circle the correct answer.

$$\boxed{\text{squeaky pop}} \qquad \boxed{\begin{array}{c}\text{turns limewater}\\\text{cloudy}\end{array}} \qquad \boxed{\begin{array}{c}\text{bleaches damp}\\\text{litmus paper}\end{array}}$$

2. In the second part of the practical, we are going to electrolyse sodium chloride solution.

a. Using the reactivity series, state which element will be produced at the cathode and explain your answer.

b. Describe how we can test for the element which is produced at the anode when we electrolyse sodium chloride
solution.

Chapter 5: Energy Changes

• Describe what is meant by an exothermic and an endothermic reaction.
• State examples of exothermic and endothermic reactions.
• Describe uses of exothermic and endothermic reactions.
• Draw and label reaction profiles for exothermic and endothermic reactions.
• Describe what is meant by the activation energy for a reaction.
• Calculate the energy change for a reaction using supplied bond energies.
• Describe how to carry out the required practical on temperature changes.
• Describe how a potential difference can be produced in a chemical cell.
• Describe the difference between a cell and a battery.
• Explain why rechargeable cells and rechargeable batteries can be recharged.
• Describe the reactions taking place in a hydrogen fuel cell.
• Evaluate the use of hydrogen fuel cells compared to rechargeable cells and batteries.
• Write half equations for the reactions taking place at the electrodes in a hydrogen fuel cell.

Exothermic and Endothermic Reactions

1. In exothermic reactions, the temperature of the surroundings increases.

a. Explain in terms of energy why the surroundings get hotter in exothermic reactions.

b. The diagrams show energy profiles for two exothermic reactions.

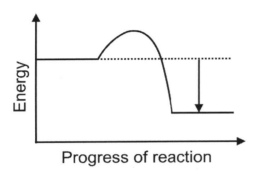

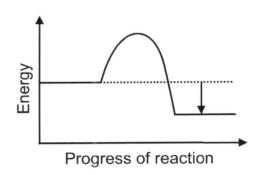

On the diagrams label the reactants, the products and the energy change.

c. State which reaction would be better for a hand-warmer and which would be better for a self-heating can of coffee. Explain your answer in each case.

d. The diagram shows an energy profile for an endothermic reaction. These are found in sports injury packs.

Explain how this shows an endothermic reaction.

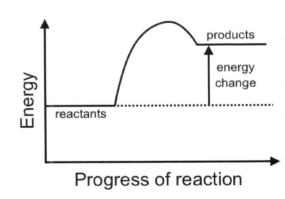

e. The activation energy is the energy needed for a reaction to occur.

Label the activation energy on the three energy profile diagrams above.

f. Label the following reactions as either exothermic or endothermic.

> oxidation

> thermal decomposition

> combustion

> neutralisation

Bond Energy Calculations 1 + 2

1. The equation below shows the reaction between iodine and chlorine gas.

Calculate the energy change using the bond energies provided.

$$I_2 \quad + \quad Cl_2 \longrightarrow 2\ ICl$$

$$I-I \qquad\qquad Cl-Cl \qquad\qquad I-Cl$$

Energy change = _____ kJ

| I — I = 151 kJ | Cl — Cl = 242 kJ | I — Cl = 208 kJ | Strictly speaking, the unit for bond energy is kJ/mol but for GCSE we simply use kJ. |

2. The equation below shows the reaction between methane and bromine.

Calculate the energy change using the bond energies provided.

$$CH_4 \quad + \quad Br_2 \longrightarrow CH_3Br \quad + \quad HBr$$

```
    H                              H
    |                              |
H − C − H      Br − Br       H − C − Br      H − Br
    |                              |
    H                              H
```

Energy change = _____ kJ

| C — H = 413 kJ | Br — Br = 193 kJ | H — Br = 366 kJ | C — Br = 276 kJ |

3. The equation below shows the reaction between nitrogen and hydrogen to form ammonia.

Calculate the energy change using the bond energies provided.

$$N_2 \quad + \quad 3H_2 \quad \rightleftharpoons \quad 2\,NH_3$$

$$N\equiv N \qquad\qquad H-H \qquad\qquad H-N-H$$
$$\underset{\qquad\qquad\qquad\qquad\qquad\qquad\qquad\qquad H}{}$$

Energy change = _____ kJ

$$N\equiv N = 941\ kJ \qquad H-H = 436\ kJ \qquad N-H = 391\ kJ$$

---

4. The equation below shows the combustion of propane.

Calculate the energy change using the bond energies provided.

$$C_3H_8 \quad + \quad 5O_2 \quad \longrightarrow \quad 3CO_2 \quad + \quad 4H_2O$$

$$\begin{array}{c} H\ \ H\ \ H \\ H-C-C-C-H \\ H\ \ H\ \ H \end{array} \qquad O=O \qquad O=C=O \qquad \begin{array}{c} O \\ H\quad H \end{array}$$

Energy change = _____ kJ

$$C-H = 413\ kJ \quad C-C = 348\ kJ \quad C=O = 799\ kJ \quad O-H = 463\ kJ \quad O=O = 495\ kJ$$

Required Practical: Temperature Changes

In this practical, we add increasing volumes of the alkali sodium hydroxide to a fixed volume of hydrochloric acid and measure the maximum temperature reached.

Exam tip: In the exam, you could be asked to describe this practical so it is worth learning the stages.

1. This reaction involves an acid and an alkali.

a. What name do scientists give to a reaction between an acid and an alkali?

b. The reaction is exothermic.

What will happen to the temperature of the solution? Explain your answer.

Temperature decreases

Temperature increases

Temperature stays the same

c. Explain why the volume of the sodium hydroxide solution is the independent variable.

d. The dependent variable is what we measure after each change in the independent variable.

What is the dependent variable in this experiment?

e. Control variables are kept the same.

State three control variables in the experiment.

f. Scientists use measuring cylinders to measure the volume of liquids.

The diagrams show the scales on two different measuring cylinders.

Which measuring cylinder would be better to use?

Explain your answer.

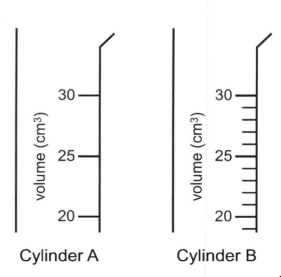

Cylinder A   Cylinder B

2. First we measure 30cm³ of hydrochloric acid into a polystyrene cup.

Explain why a measuring cylinder is better for measuring volume than using a beaker.

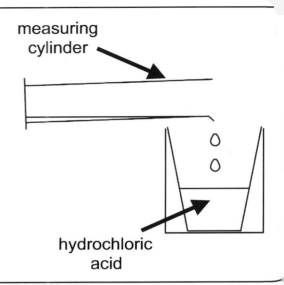

measuring cylinder

hydrochloric acid

thermometer

3. Next we use a thermometer to measure the temperature of the acid.

We record this starting temperature in a results table.

Different students can read the same thermometer but get slightly different results.

What name do scientists give to this type of error?

Systematic Error

Human Error

Random Error

4. Now we use a measuring cylinder to add 5cm³ of sodium hydroxide solution.

We stir the reaction and measure the highest temperature reached.

a. Suggest why it is important that we stir the reaction.

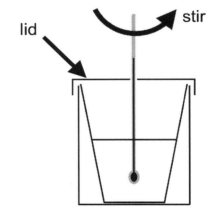

lid

stir

b. Explain why we use a polystyrene cup with a lid for this experiment rather than simply a glass beaker.

We now carry out the experiment several times, increasing the volume of sodium hydroxide solution. We then repeat the whole experiment and calculate mean values for the temperature increases.

5. The results of the experiment are shown in the table below.

Volume of sodium hydroxide solution (cm³)	Temperature increase (°C) Repeat One	Temperature increase (°C) Repeat Two	Mean temperature increase (°C)
5	2	2	2.0
10	4	5	4.5
15	7	8	7.5
20	8	7	7.5
25	10	11	10.5
30	13	12	12.5
35	12	10	11.0
40	10	9	9.5

a. Plot the data on the axes below and draw two lines of best fit.

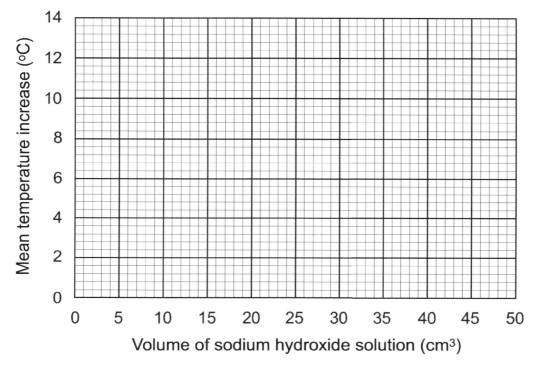

b. What conclusions can we make from the results of this experiment?

c. Use the idea of limiting reactant to explain why the temperature increase falls after 30 cm³ of sodium hydroxide.

d. Use your graph to predict the temperature increase that would take place if 23 cm³ of sodium hydroxide solution was used.

6. It is important to check your data for anomalous results.

a. A student stated "I think that repeat two for 20 cm³ is an anomalous result".

Use the results to explain why the student may have stated this.

b. Suggest an error that the student may have made that could have led to this anomalous result.

c. What should the student do with the anomalous result?

7. Whenever a measurement is made, there is always some uncertainty about the result obtained.

We can estimate the size of the uncertainty by using the range of a set of numbers about the mean.

Two students decided to check the results for 20 cm³ of sodium hydroxide solution.

Their results are shown in the two tables below.

Student A

Temperature increase (°C)			
Repeat 1	Repeat 2	Repeat 3	Mean
8	10	9	9.0

Student B

Temperature increase (°C)			
Repeat 1	Repeat 2	Repeat 3	Mean
7	12	8	9.0

a. The range is the minimum and maximum values for a set of results.

State the range of the results generated by student A and student B.

> Student A

> Student B

b. Which set of results show the greatest uncertainty?

Explain your answer.

Cells and Batteries

1. The diagram below shows two metals in a solution of copper sulfate.

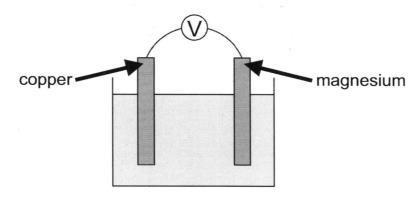

a. The electrolyte is a solution that conducts electricity.

Label the electrolyte on the diagram above.

b. What name do scientists give to a setup such as the one shown in the diagram?

| A hydrogen fuel cell | A battery | A cell |

c. Magnesium is a more reactive metal than copper.

Magnesium atoms lose electrons to form magnesium ions.

Complete the half equation to show the number of electrons lost by the magnesium atoms.

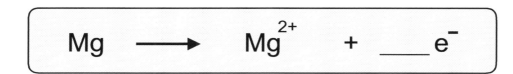

$$Mg \longrightarrow Mg^{2+} + \underline{}\, e^-$$

d. Is the above reaction an example of oxidation or reduction?

Explain your answer.

e. Draw an arrow on the diagram to show the direction that the electric current (the flow of electrons) will travel.

f. Explain why a setup such as the one above can only generate electricity for a limited amount of time.

2. The diagram below shows two different cells.

In both cells, the electrolyte is the same.

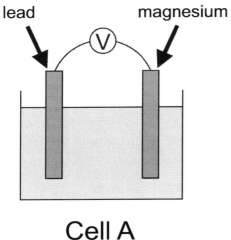

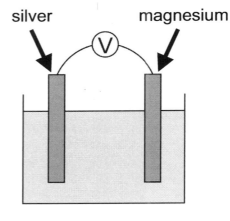

a. Use the reactivity series to predict which of the two cells will have the greatest potential difference and the greatest current.

Explain your answer.

b. Why is it important that the electrolyte is the same in both cases?

c. The diagram shows two cells connected in series.

The potential difference generated by each cell is 1.5 V.

What will be the overall potential difference?

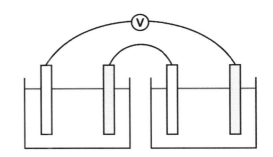

d. What name do scientists give to cells connected in series?

e. Alkaline batteries cannot be recharged.

At some point one of the reactants is used up and the potential difference falls to zero.

Other types of batteries can be recharged.

Explain how some batteries can be recharged.

Fuel Cells

When hydrogen reacts with oxygen, the reaction is strongly exothermic and a great deal of energy is released. In a fuel cell, this energy is released gradually as an electric current.

1. The hydrogen fuel cell consists of four stages (you need to learn these).

Stage 1. Hydrogen atoms are oxidised on one side, releasing electrons.

Stage 2. The electrons now make their way around a circuit as an electric current. The energy carried by the electrons can be used to power appliances connected into the circuit.

Stage 3. The hydrogen ions move to the other side of the fuel cell.

Stage 4. The electrons and hydrogen ions combine with oxygen atoms to make water as a waste product.

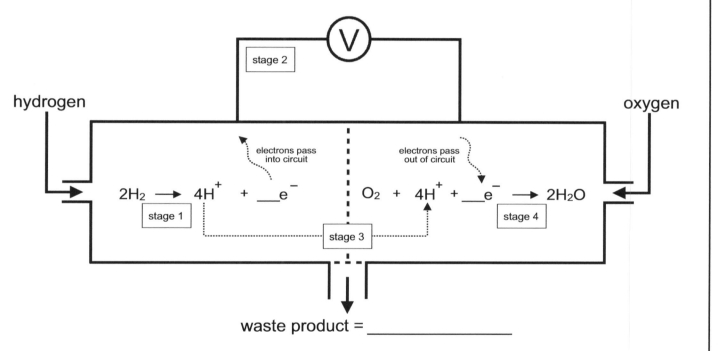

waste product = _____

a. Complete the half equations to show the number of electrons transferred.

b. Draw an arrow to show the direction of the electric current (negative to positive).

c. Complete the diagram to show the waste product.

d. In the fuel cell, hydrogen is oxidised.

Explain how this is shown by the half equation in stage 1.

2. The equation below shows the reaction between hydrogen and oxygen in a fuel cell.

Use the bond energies to calculate the energy released by the reaction.

You have seen the structures already in the topic on covalent bonding.

$$2H_2 \quad + \quad O_2 \quad \longrightarrow \quad 2\,H_2O$$

Energy change = _____ kJ

$H-H = 436$ kJ $O-H = 463$ kJ $O=O = 495$ kJ

---

3. In the exam, you could be asked to evaluate the use of hydrogen fuel cells in comparison with rechargeable cells and batteries.

a. Complete the table to show the advantages and disadvantages of these.

Hydrogen Fuel Cells	Rechargeable Cells and Batteries
Hydrogen fuel cells will produce electricity for as long as you provide hydrogen	
	Rechargeable batteries can store less electricity the more charging cycles they go through and eventually need replacing
Hydrogen gas is explosive and difficult to store safely	
	Rechargeable batteries can produce a much greater potential difference than hydrogen fuel cells

b. Describe how the waste water produced by a hydrogen fuel cell can be useful.

Chemistry Paper 1

GCSE Specimen Paper

Time allowed: 105 minutes

Maximum marks: 100

Please note that this is a specimen exam paper written by freesciencelessons. The questions are meant to reflect the style of questions that you might see in your GCSE Chemistry exam.

Neither the exam paper nor the mark scheme have been endorsed by any exam board. The answers are my best estimates of what would be accepted but I cannot guarantee that this would be the case. I do not offer any guarantee that the level you achieve in this specimen paper is the level that you will achieve in the real exam.

1   When metals react with acids, energy changes can take place.

1.1   Complete the balanced equation to show the reaction between iron and hydrochloric acid.

                                  1 mark

$$Fe \quad + \quad \underline{\hspace{3cm}} \quad \longrightarrow \quad FeCl_2 \quad + \quad H_2$$

1.2   Iron chloride ($FeCl_2$) contains the chloride ion Cl^-

           Give the charge on the iron ion.

                                  1 mark

_____

1.3   Describe a method to investigate the energy change when different masses of iron are reacted with hydrochloric acid.

           Your method should produce valid results.

                                  6 marks

_____

_____

_____

_____

_____

_____

_____

_____

_____

_____

_____

_____

You may continue your answer on the following page.

Total = 8

2   This question is about metals in group 1 of the periodic table.

2 . 1   The element lithium is found in group 1.

Lithium consists of two common isotopes.

Figure 1 shows the structure of one of the isotopes of lithium.

Figure 1

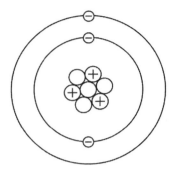

Explain how the diagram shows that lithium must be in group 1 of the periodic table.

1 mark

_____

2 . 2   The other isotope of lithium has the symbol $^{6}_{3}\text{Li}$

Describe one difference between this isotope and the isotope shown in figure 1.

Your answer should refer to sub-atomic particles.

2 marks

_____

_____

_____

Question 2 continues on the next page.

2.3   Explain why elements in group 1 cannot be extracted using carbon.

2 marks

_____

_____

_____

_____

2.4   Lithium is found in the compound lithium chloride.

Figure 2 shows the ball and stick diagram for lithium chloride.

Figure 2

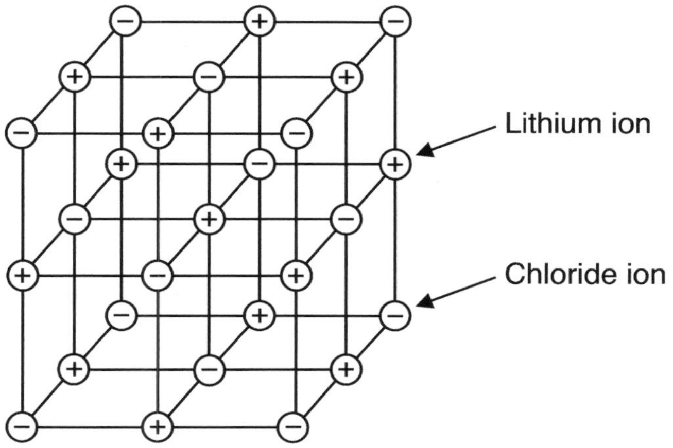

Lithium chloride melts at around 610°C.

Explain why lithium chloride has a high melting point.

2 marks

_____

_____

_____

2.5   Describe one limitation of ball and stick diagrams such as the one above.

1 mark

_____

_____

2.6   Sodium is below lithium in group 1.

Explain why sodium is more reactive than lithium.

3 marks

_____

_____

_____

_____

_____

_____

_____

_____

_____

Total = 11

3   This question is about separating mixtures.

3 . 1   A scientist wanted to separate a mixture of three different alcohols.

Table 1 shows the boiling points of the alcohols.

Table 1

Alcohol	Molecular formula	Boiling points (^{o}C)
Methanol	CH_3OH	65
Ethanol	C_2H_5OH	78
Butanol	C_4H_9OH	118

Describe the link between the number of carbon atoms and the boiling point.

1 mark

_____

_____

3 . 2   The alcohol propanol has the molecular formula C_3H_7OH.

Predict the boiling point of propanol.

1 mark

_____

3 . 3   Which type of bonding is found in molecules containing only non-metals.

1 mark

Tick **one** box.

Covalent		**Metallic**		**Ionic**	

Question 3 continues on the next page.

3 . 4   **Figure 3** shows the equipment used by the scientist to separate the alcohols.

Figure 3

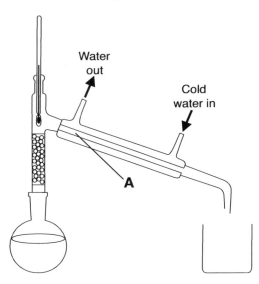

State the name of the process that uses the above apparatus.

1 mark

_____

3 . 5   Describe what is taking place in part A.

2 marks

_____

_____

_____

3 . 6   Explain why the scientist is more likely to produce a pure sample of butanol rather than methanol or ethanol.   **2 marks**

_____

_____

_____

Total = 8

4   This question is about the reactions of acids.

4.1   The reaction between copper carbonate and sulfuric acid is shown below.

Complete the equation to show the missing products of the reaction.

2 marks

copper   +   sulfuric   copper   +   _____   +   _____
carbonate   acid   sulfate

4.2   A scientist wanted to make 200 cm³ of 0.1 mol / dm³ sulfuric acid (H_2SO_4).
Calculate the mass of sulfuric acid required to make this.

Relative atomic masses (Ar): $H = 1$ $S = 32$ $O = 16$

You **must** show your working.

4 marks

_____

_____

_____

_____

_____

                                          Mass = _____ g

4.3   Describe a method to make pure, dry crystals of copper sulfate using powdered copper carbonate and dilute sulfuric acid.

6 marks

_____

_____

_____

_____

_____

_____

_____

_____

_____

_____

_____

_____

_____

_____

_____

_____

_____

_____

Total = 1

5   Aluminium can be produced by electrolysis of molten aluminium oxide and the chemical cryolite.

Figure 4 shows the apparatus.

Figure 4

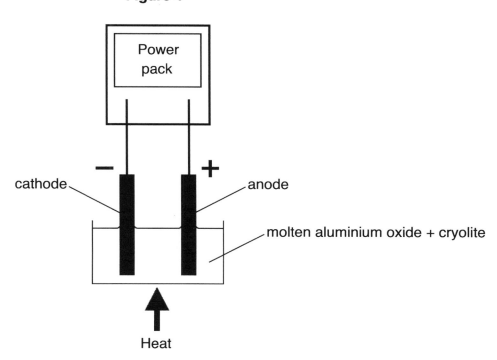

5.1   Explain why the aluminium oxide must be molten.

2 marks

_____

_____

_____

5.2   Why is cryolite added to the aluminium oxide?

2 marks

_____

_____

_____

5.3   During electrolysis, aluminium ions gain electrons at the cathode.

What name do scientists give to a reaction where electrons are gained?

1 mark

_____

5.4   Complete the half equation to show the reaction taking place at the cathode.

2 marks

$$Al^{3+} \quad + \quad \underline{\quad} e^- \quad \longrightarrow \quad \underline{\qquad}$$

5.5   The electrodes are made of graphite.

Explain why the anode must be replaced regularly?

3 marks

_____

_____

_____

_____

_____

5.6   Give two reasons why producing aluminium using electrolysis is very expensive.

2 marks

Reason 1 _____

_____

_____

Reason 2 _____

_____

_____

Total = 1?

6 Elements in group 7 of the periodic table are used extensively in Chemistry.

6.1 Give the name that scientists use for group 7.

1 mark

_____

6.2 Explain why all of the elements in group 7 have similar reactions.

1 mark

_____

6.3 The element chlorine is in group 7.

Chlorine reacts rapidly with group 1 elements such as sodium.

Complete the equation to show the reaction between chlorine and sodium.

3 marks

2Na   +   _____   ⟶   _____

6.4 The reaction of chlorine with group 1 elements is exothermic.

Draw and label a reaction profile for the reaction between chlorine and sodium on **figure 5**.

4 marks

Figure 5

Progress of reaction

6.5 Elements in group 7 form diatomic molecules eg Cl_2.

State the type of chemical bonding found in these molecules.

1 mark

_____

_____

6.6 When chlorine reacts, it can form the chloride ion (Cl^-) as follows.

$$Cl_2 \quad + \quad 2\,e^- \quad \longrightarrow \quad 2\,Cl^-$$

Calculate the number of chloride ions produced when 71g of chlorine (Cl_2) react.

Give your answer in standard form to 3 significant figures.

The value of Avogadro's constant is 6.02×10^{23}

Relative atomic masses (Ar): $Cl = 35.5$

4 marks

_____

_____

_____

_____

_____

_____

_____

_____

_____

_____

number of chloride ions = _____

Total = 1

7   The element oxygen is in group 6.

7.1   Complete the dot and cross diagram to show the covalent bonding in an oxygen molecule O_2.

Show only electrons in the outer energy level.

2 marks

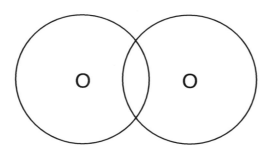

7.2   Oxygen can be produced by decomposing hydrogen peroxide (H_2O_2).

The equation for this reaction is:

$$2\,H_2O_2 \longrightarrow 2\,H_2O + O_2$$

Calculate the mass of hydrogen peroxide required to make 2.4 dm³ of oxygen (assume the reaction takes place at room temperature and pressure).

Relative atomic masses (A_r):   H = 1   O = 16

You **must** show your working.

4 marks

_____

_____

_____

_____

_____

_____

_____

Mass = _____ g

7.3 Suggest two reasons why the amount of product in a chemical reaction may be less than the amount predicted.

2 marks

_____

_____

_____

_____

7.4 The displayed formula for the reaction of hydrogen peroxide is shown below.

$$2 \quad \overset{O-O}{\underset{H \qquad H}{}} \quad \longrightarrow \quad 2 \quad \overset{O}{\underset{H \quad H}{}} \quad + \quad O=O$$

	O — H	O — O	O = O
Energy (kJ / mol)	463	146	495

Use the bond energies to calculate the overall energy change for this reaction.

3 marks

_____

_____

_____

_____

_____

_____

_____

_____

Energy change = _____ kJ / mol

Total = 1

8   This question is about acids and alkalis.

8 . 1   Ethanoic acid (CH_3COOH) ionises in water.

The equation for this reaction is shown below:

$$CH_3COOH \rightleftharpoons CH_3COO^- + H^+$$

Explain how this shows that ethanoic acid is a weak acid.

2 marks

_____

_____

_____

8 . 2   A sample of ethanoic acid had a pH of 5.

Water was added to the sample to produce a more dilute solution.

Explain how this would affect the pH.

2 marks

_____

_____

8 . 3   A sample of ethanoic acid had a pH of 5.

Another solution has a concentration of H+ which is two orders of magnitude greater.

State the pH of this solution and explain your answer.

3 marks

pH of the solution = _____

_____

_____

_____

_____

8 . 4   A student used titration to find the concentration of a solution of hydrochloric acid.

In each titration, they used 25 cm³ of 0.15 mol / dm³ calcium hydroxide solution.

The mean value for the volume of hydrochloric acid used was 22.5 cm³.

The equation for the reaction is:

$$Ca(OH)_2 \ + \ 2\,HCl \longrightarrow CaCl_2 \ + \ 2\,H_2O$$

Calculate the concentration of the hydrochloric acid in mol / dm³.

3 marks

_____

_____

_____

_____

_____

_____

_____

_____

_____

Concentration of hydrochloric acid = _____ mol / dm³

8.5 Explain why a pipette can be used to measure the volume of calcium hydroxide solution but not to measure the volume of hydrochloric acid.

2 marks

_____

_____

_____

_____

8.6 In the titration, the student used the indicator methyl orange.

Explain the advantage of using an indicator such as methyl orange compared to universal indicator.

3 marks

_____

_____

_____

_____

_____

_____

_____

_____

8.7 The reaction between any acid and any alkali is an example of neutralisation.

Give the equation for neutralisation.

1 mark

_____

Total = 16

9   In 1904, the scientist J.J. Thomson proposed an early model of atomic structure.

Scientists at the time called this the "plum pudding model".

9.1   Describe the main features of the plum-pudding model.

2 marks

_____

_____

9.2   In 1909, the scientists Geiger and Marsden carried out the
alpha-scattering experiment.

Describe the alpha-scattering experiment and how the results led to the
development of the nuclear model of atomic structure.

5 marks

_____

_____

_____

_____

_____

_____

_____

_____

_____

9.3   Explain how Niels Bohr contributed to the development of the nuclear model.

1 mark

_____

_____

End of questions

Total = 8

Printed in Great Britain
by Amazon